THE TERM STRUCTURE
OF INTEREST RATES

THE TERM STRUCTURE

Basic Books, Inc. Publishers

NEW YORK   LONDON

OF INTEREST RATES

Charles R. Nelson

Library of Congress Catalog Card Number: 77-174822
SBN 465-08409-5
Manufactured in the United States of America

To My Parents

Foreword

Contributions to the economics of uncertainty have become much more frequent and significant in the last twenty years. Powerful impetus has come from the development of mathematical statistics and of probability theory and from the confluence of economic and statistical considerations known as decision theory. The influences between the fields have been reciprocal and sometimes unexpected. The practical statistician, engaged, for example, in acceptance inspection or quality control, is in part a decision-maker, and the economic aspects in these decisions became abundantly clear to such contributors as E. C. Molina, W. A. Shewhart, and their associates at Bell Telephone Laboratories in the 1920s and 1930s. Gradually this attitude, reflected especially in the seminal work of Jerzy Neyman, permeated the higher reaches of statistical theory and reached an elegant formulation in the explicit and general introduction of economic choice at the very foundations of statistical theory by Abraham Wald about 1945. In Wald's case, of course, the direct influence of economic theory can be traced with no difficulty to his earlier work in mathematical economics. This direction of research was made more fruitful with the acceptance of Bernoulli's eighteenth-century expected-utility hypothesis of behavior under uncertainty, always known to theoretical economists but regarded with some suspicion by the ordinalists; now the new axiomatic formulations of John von Neumann and Oskar Morgenstern and of Leonard J. Savage (1944, 1954) made Bernoulli's hypothesis acceptable (Ramsey's earlier similar achievement had been overlooked completely).

The expected-utility hypothesis has at least one virtue; it is capable of both easy interpretation and fruitful manipulation to achieve conclusions. In particular, the concept of risk aversion cannot only be easily defined but can be analyzed and related to behavior, and more specific hypotheses can be formulated with relative ease. Thus, in the field covered by Dr. Nelson's distinguished study, the rather vague idea that the difference between long and short interest rates contains a premium for uncertainty can be translated into fairly specific hypotheses, capable of being tested. In particular, he draws the interesting conclusion that, other things being equal, the term premium should be less, the higher the interest rate.

Another relevant development of mathematical statistics and probability theory during the last forty years has been the virtual creation of specific methods of time series analysis. Since economics itself involves time in an intrinsic way, empirical economists had found it necessary to develop their own tools for the analysis of observations over time until more sophisticated methods were developed by the probability theorists. After Kolmogorov's early work, Herman Wold early grasped the central themes of time series analysis and developed them in the late 1930s. Since World War II, theoretical developments and the practical needs of communications engineering have led to both deeper developments in pure theory and the practical methods of spectral analysis. The characteristic effects of different kinds of time dependencies (stochastic processes) on the spectrum and the correlogram, already studied by Wold, are heavily exploited by Dr. Nelson in the following study. Economics now returns the compliment paid by theoretical statistics; the statistician having become an economic man, the economic agent is now seen as an optimal statistician, projecting the future of interest rates from a determination of the stochastic process underlying their past.

Dr. Nelson has shown the value of these new tools to one of the classical problems of economics, the determination of the term structure of interest rates. This problem is clearly important enough practically to be worth all the attention that has been paid to it and more, but it is also very important from the theoretical viewpoint. While all economic behavior is influenced by expectations of the future, the markets for loans of varying maturities are virtually the only ones that offer some possibility of separating expectations from other factors in the decision. The fact, then, that agents appear on these markets to be good forecasters operating under risk aversion may encourage carrying over these hypotheses to, say, the demand for fixed investment.

No doubt, much remains to be done, and Dr. Nelson has himself indicated illuminatingly possible directions for future research. But the thoroughness of his work and the skill with which he has employed his sophisticated tools make this study an enduring contribution to the field.

KENNETH J. ARROW

Harvard University

Preface

This volume is the second winner of the Irving Fisher Award Series, sponsored by Omicron Delta Epsilon, the International Honor Society in Economics. The author of the volume, Professor Charles Nelson of the University of Chicago, won the Irving Fisher Award in competition with other graduate students and recent Ph.D.s. Each entry was first judged by a selection committee in the entrant's own department, with the winner moving to one of nine regional selection boards. The regional winners were entered in the finals and judged by the final selection board, composed of Professors Kenneth J. Arrow, Kenneth E. Boulding, Milton Friedman, Paul Samuelson, and Egon Neuberger (*ex officio*). I am grateful to the many eminent economists serving on the selection boards, without whose unstinting work this series would not have been possible.

I am delighted that the Irving Fisher competition caught on as quickly as it did and that the entries were of exceptionally high quality. All those who entered the competitions are to be congratulated.

I wish to thank all the other contributors to the success of the Irving Fisher Award competition, particularly Professors Ervin K. Zingler, President of ODE; Alan A. Brown, Chairman of the Board of Trustees of ODE; members of the ODE Executive Committee; Martin Kessler, Senior Editor of Basic

Books, Inc.; and Richard Dusansky, Associate Editor of the Award Series.

Professor Kenneth J. Arrow continues the tradition initiated by Professor Paul A. Samuelson last year when he wrote a foreword to the 1970 winner of the Irving Fisher Award, *The Behavior of Interest Rates: The Application of the Efficient Market Model to U.S. Treasury Bills* by Richard Roll. Professor Arrow performs a great service by placing the present volume within the context of recent developments in economic theory and I strongly advise the reader to refer to his foreword before reading the book.

I hope that all those qualified to participate in the competition will regard this book as a challenge to enter and that all senior members of the profession will consider it as an invitation to encourage their students and younger colleagues to participate. I am hoping that both the quantity and quality of entries will continue to rise, making not only the first but also the second derivative positive.

EGON   NEUBERGER
Editor
Irving Fisher Award Series

Acknowledgments

This study was initiated while I was a resident student at the University of Wisconsin and was completed during a postdoctoral year at the University of Chicago.

I owe a large debt to Arthur S. Goldberger, the chairman of my thesis committee, for his encouragement, guidance, and very generous allocation of time. His numerous comments and suggestions have added much to the content and exposition of this study.

Other members of my thesis committee, Edgar Feige, Donald Hester, Donald Nicholas, and George Tiao, also provided helpful criticism. James Taylor of the Social Systems Research Institute at the University of Wisconsin wrote the computer programs for the analysis of time series used in this study and assisted in solving various other computational problems. I was supported at the University of Wisconsin by the Richard D. Irwin Foundation.

I have also benefited from the criticism of my colleagues at the University of Chicago, notably Zvi Griliches, Reuben Kessel, Lester Telser, and Arnold Zellner. I am particularly indebted to Merton Miller for many insightful and constructive comments. I was supported at the University of Chicago during the course of this study by a postdoctoral fellowship from the Graduate School of Business.

Various drafts of this manuscript were typed accurately and efficiently under the supervision of Mrs. Ilene Haniotis.

The editors of the *Journal of the American Statistical Association* have kindly given permission to reproduce materials that originally appeared there.

Contents

1

INTRODUCTION   1

2

**PRELIMINARIES: MEASUREMENT OF THE TERM
STRUCTURE, FORWARD INTEREST RATES, AND
DISCRETE LINEAR STOCHASTIC PROCESSES**   3

Problems in the Measurement of the Term Structure   3
Futures Market Implicit in the Term Structure   6
Discrete Linear Stochastic Processes   9

3

**THEORIES OF THE TERM STRUCTURE OF INTEREST
RATES AND THE METHODOLOGY OF EMPIRICAL TESTS**   18

Traditional Expectations Theory   18
Liquidity Preference Theory   20
Preferred Habitat Theory   28
Hedging Pressure Theory   30
Meiselman's Error-learning Model   31
Cyclical Movement of Liquidity Premiums   33
Summary and Conclusions   36

4

MODEL OF THE CYCLICAL MOVEMENT OF THE TERM STRUCTURE OF INTEREST RATES   39

Introduction   39

Forward Loans and Expected Utility   40

Response to Changes in the Term Premium: Income and Substitution Effects   46

Response to Changes in the Level of Interest Rates   52

Speculators and Future Borrowers   56

Net Supply of Forward Loans   59

Aggregation of Individual Supply Functions   60

Measurement of Market Expectations   64

5

REPRESENTATION OF THE DURAND ANNUAL ONE-YEAR RATES AS A DISCRETE LINEAR STOCHASTIC PROCESS   66

Introduction   66

Identification of Linear Process Models and Estimation of Parameters   67

Application of the Identification Procedure to the Durand One-year Spot Rates   70

Estimation of Parameters   77

Computation of Conditional Expectations   82

6

TESTING THE TERM-PREMIUM MODEL BY SIMULATION OF MARKET EXPECTATIONS   85

Introduction   85

Description of Data Used in Tests of the Term-premium Model   86

Estimation of Parameters in the Term-premium Model   89
Check on the Specification of $_t\widehat{T}_{t+n}$ 94
Test of the Specification of I_t and Z_t as Determinants
    of Term Premiums   96
Predictive Content of Time Series Forecasts and of
    I_t and Z_t 99
Test of the Liquidity Preference Theory   104

7

**TEST OF THE TERM-PREMIUM MODEL IN AN
ERROR-LEARNING FRAMEWORK   107**
Introduction   107
Reassessment of Evidence for the Expectations Theory
    from the Error-learning Model   108
Term-premium Model in the Error-learning Framework   112

8

SUMMARY AND SUGGESTIONS FOR FURTHER RESEARCH   117
Summary   117
Suggestions for Further Research   119

BIBLIOGRAPHY   121
INDEX   124

Tables

5-1 The Durand One-year Maturity Spot Interest Rates and Conditional Expectations Computed from AR(2) and IMA(1,1) for Origin Dates, 1900–1967   72

5-2 Comparison of Parameter Estimates   80

6-1 Yields on Commercial Paper, I_t, and Unemployment Rate, Z_t, 1901–1958   88

6-2 Estimates of Parameters in the Model $_t\widehat{T}_{t+n} = a_n + b_n I_t + c_n Z_t + \epsilon_{n,t}$ Using AR(2) Conditional Expectations, 1901–1958   90

6-3 Estimates of Parameters in the Model $_t\widehat{T}_{t+n} = a_n + b_n I_t + c_n Z_t + \epsilon_{n,t}$ Using IMA(1,1) Conditional Expectations, 1901–1958   91

6-4 Efficient Estimates of Parameters in the Model $_t\widehat{T}^T_{t+n} = a^T_n + b_n I^T_t + c_n Z^T_t + \gamma_{n,t}$ Using AR(2) and IMA(1,1) Conditional Expectations, 1903–1958   93

6-5 Estimates in Parameters in the Model $_t r_{t+n} = a_n + b_n I_t + c_n Z_t + d_{nt}\widehat{R}^*_{t+n} + \epsilon_{n,t}$ Using AR(2) and IMA(1,1) Conditional Expectations, 1901–1958   95

6-6 Estimates of Parameters in the Model $_t r_{t+n} - R_{t+n} = a_n + b_n I_t + c_n Z_t + (f_{n,t} - \delta_{n,t})$, 1900–1958   98

6-7 Estimates in the Parameters in the Regressions $R_{t+n} = a^0_n + d^0_{nt}\widehat{R}^*_{t+n} + \delta^0_{n,t}$ Using AR(2) and IMA(1,1) Conditional Expectations, 1901–1958   101

6-8   Estimates of the Parameters in the Models $R_{t+n} = a_n^* + b_n^* I_t + c_n^* Z_t + d_{nt}^* \widehat{R}_{t+n}^* + (\epsilon_{n,t}^* + \delta_{n,t})$ Using AR(2) and IMA(1,1) Conditional Expectations, 1901–1958   103

6-9   Estimates of the Parameters in the Models $R_{t+n} = -a_n' - b_n' I_t - c_n' Z_t + d_{nt}' r_{t+n} + \delta_{n,t}$, 1901–1958   105

7-1   Estimates of Parameters in the Model $_t r_{t+n} - {}_{t-1} r_{t+n} = (a_n' - a_{n+1}' + \psi_n a_1') + \psi_n (R_t - {}_{t-1} r_t) + [(w_{n,t}' - w_{n+1,t-1}' + \psi_n w_{1,t-1}) + (f_{n,t}' - f_{n+1,t+1}' + \psi_n f_{1,t-1})]$, 1901–1958   110

7-2   Values of $\widehat{\widehat{\psi}}_n$ Implied by Estimated AR(2) and IMA(1,1) Models and Discrepancies from $\widehat{\psi}_n$ 111

7-3   Estimates of Parameters in the Model $_t r_{t+n} - {}_{t-1} r_{t+n} = \alpha_n + \psi_n (R_t - {}_{t-1} r_t) + b_n I_t + (\psi_n b_1 - b_{n+1}) I_{t-1} + c_n Z_t + (\psi_n c_1 - c_{n+1}) Z_{t-1} + (W_{n,t} + F_{n,t})$, 1901–1958   113

7-4   Restricted Efficient Estimates of Parameters in the Model $_t r_{t+n} - {}_{t-1} r_{t+n} = \alpha_n + \psi_n (R_t - {}_{t-1} r_t) + b_n I_t + B_n I_{t-1} + c_n Z_t + C_n Z_{t-1} + (W_{n,t} + F_{n,t})$, 1901–1958   115

Figures

4–1 Income and Substitution Effects, $T > 0$ 47

4–2 Income and Substitution Effects, $T < 0$ 50

4–3 Response of Future Lenders to Rise in Level of
Interest Rates 55

4–4 Response of Future Borrowers to Rise in Level of
Interest Rates 58

5–1 Sample Autocorrelations of Durand Annual
One-year Spot Rates, 1900–1965 71

5–2 Sample Autocorrelations of First Differences of
Annual Durand One-year Spot Rates, 1900–1965 74

5–3 Ninety-percent Confidence Region for Parameters
ϕ_1 and ϕ_2 for Model AR(2) 78

THE TERM STRUCTURE
OF INTEREST RATES

Introduction

    Although economists speak loosely of "the interest rate," there is, in fact, a wide spectrum of rates prevailing at any given time. This variation in interest rates is related, presumably, to the special characteristics of the different interest-bearing obligations in question. One might expect that among the most important determinants of the relations among market yields of different securities would be default risk, tax features, marketability, and term to maturity. The functional relationship between yield and term to maturity for securities that are homogeneous with respect to other relevant characteristics is called the term structure of interest rates. The objective of this study is to develop and test a model of the movement of the term structure through time.

    The content of this study may be outlined as follows. Chapter 2 discusses the empirical measurement of the term structure and describes the data that are available for U.S. bond markets. Chapter 2 also contains an introduction to the theory of discrete linear stochastic processes, which will form the basis for our theoretical and empirical treatment of the role of expectations in the determination of the term structure. Chapter 3 reviews the principal themes in the development of theories of the term structure and discusses problems that have been encountered in empirical testing. We examine there in detail the proposition that the positive average slope of yield curves during the twentieth century constitutes evidence for the existence of liquidity premiums.

Chapter 4 describes a model of the term structure that arises from consideration of the maturity-choice problem facing risk-averse market participants seeking to maximize expected utility. The analysis suggests that the forward interest rates implicit in the term structure consist of the corresponding expected future spot rate plus a *term premium* that varies inversely with the level of interest rates and with an index of business confidence. Tests of the term-premium model focus on the use of conditional expectations implied by discrete linear stochastic processes as simulated values of market expectations. Particular processes are identified and fitted in Chapter 5 as models for the one-year Durand rates. Regressions of estimated term premiums on measures of the level of interest rates and business confidence are employed in Chapter 6 to obtain estimates of parameters in the term-premium model. Further tests are designed to check on the empirical specification of the simulated market expectations and the variables representing determinants of term premiums. Finally, in Chapter 7, the term-premium model is tested in an error-learning framework.

A summary of our findings and suggestions for further research are presented in Chapter 8.

Preliminaries: Measurement of the Term Structure, Forward Interest Rates, and Discrete Linear Stochastic Processes

PROBLEMS IN THE MEASUREMENT OF THE TERM STRUCTURE

Consider a class of securities that are homogeneous with respect to their relevant characteristics except for term to maturity. Future payments associated with any of these securities are presumably discounted in the market by a set of interest rates appropriate to the periods of payment. Hence, if $R_{n,t}$ is the interest rate by which the market in period t discounts payments to be received n periods in the future, then for the current market price P_t of a bond offering coupon payments C_i i periods in the future and for the terminal payment A_n n periods in the future, we have

$$P_t = \frac{C_1}{1 + R_{1,t}} + \frac{C_2}{(1 + R_{2,t})^2} + \cdots + \frac{C_n + A_n}{(1 + R_{n,t})^n}. \quad (2.1)$$

The set of yields, $R_{1,t}, R_{2,t}, \ldots,$ is the term structure of interest rates in period t for this homogeneous group of securities.

To correspond with our definition of the term structure, market yields should be measured as the market rate of discount on a single payment to be made at some future date. In practice, however, yields are computed as the *yield to maturity*, a single rate that discounts the stream of coupon payments and the terminal payment of a bond to the market price. The yield to maturity, then, is the single rate, say $R'_{n,t}$, that discounts the payment stream to P_t so that it satisfies

$$P_t = \frac{C_1}{1 + R'_{n,t}} + \frac{C_2}{(1 + R'_{n,t})^2} + \cdots + \frac{A_n + C_n}{(1 + R'_{n,t})^n}. \quad (2.2)$$

Clearly, there is no reason to expect that $R'_{n,t}$ computed in this way should be the same as $R_{n,t}$. In fact, $R'_{n,t}$ will be a complex mixture of the $R_{i,t}$, with the relative weights depending on the C_i. Note that in the special case that all $C_i = 0$; indeed, $R'_{n,t} = R_{n,t}$. In general, yields to maturity will vary between bonds of the same maturity if they differ in coupon payments. Further, the concept of maturity itself is imprecise for bonds with coupon payments, since there is a sequence of payments, with the face value paid at *maturity* merely being the final payment. We may view a bond, then, as a collection of future payments of various maturities.

The available term-structure data have been constructed from yields to maturity as computed in (2.2) and necessarily differ from the structure of yields on single-payment future receipts. Since it is the latter set of yields to which theories of the term structure have pertained, it has been necessary in empirical work to rely on market-yield data as an approximation to single-payment yields. Wallace concluded that for coupons of the size usually encountered in practice, the errors in market yields as approximations to the term structure may be small relative to other errors in measurement.[1] Malkiel analyzed the problem in detail and presents calculated discrepancies for hypothetical coupon sizes.[2]

When market yields for a homogeneous group of securities are plotted on a graph with yield on the ordinate and term to maturity on the abscissa, typically a scatter of points is obtained. A curve fitted through this scatter is known as the yield curve for the given market date. The scattering of observations is presumably due to factors such as using yields to maturity on bonds that differ in coupon payments and the fact that the securities in the group are not precisely homogeneous. In practice, term-structure data consist of the smoothed yields read off the yield curve. Henceforth, the symbol $R_{i,t}$ will denote these yields, where the first subscript denotes term to maturity and the second the market date. When the first subscript is omitted, a one-period yield is understood.

Two sets of yield curve data for the United States are available. An annual series of high-grade corporate bond yields for the years 1900–1958 has been developed by Durand.[3] Durand fitted the curves by freehand as envelopes under the lowest (and hence presumably least subject to default risk) yields in a scatter of yields to maturity for a large number of high-grade corporate issues. Durand constrained the fitted curves to be monotonic. No "humped" shapes were allowed. While this series is referred to as "default free," that description is probably not quite accurate, since corporate yields have consistently been above U.S. Treasury yields of the same maturities.

Yield curves for U.S. Treasury securities have been fitted on a monthly basis since 1939 by the U.S. Treasury Department.[4] The curves are fitted freehand through the scatter of prevailing yields. Issues that have characteristics such as call features that make a comparison of yield to maturity ambiguous are generally ignored. Unlike the Durand curves, the Treasury curves include irregular hump shapes. A variety of shortcomings render these yield curves generally unusable for years prior to 1954. Contributing to this deficiency are a scarcity of certain maturities, call features, exchange privileges, and the like.[5]

FUTURES MARKET IMPLICIT IN THE TERM STRUCTURE

The presence in the bond market of an array of maturities opens to participants the opportunity for securing either loans or investments for future periods. For example, by selling a no-coupon ten-period bond and buying a no-coupon twenty-period bond, a ten-period investment may in effect be secured to begin ten periods hence at a rate of interest set by the spot market in long-term securities. The rate of interest on such a forward loan or investment may be computed as follows. Taking $n > k$, the investor who at the beginning of period t simultaneously buys an n-period bond and sells a k-period bond will pay out $(1 + R_{k,t})^k$ at the end of k periods and will receive $(1 + R_{n,t})^n$ at the end of n periods. Then the rate of return for the $n - k$ periods, which discounts the receipt, $(1 + R_{n,t})^n$, to the cost, $(1 + R_{k,t})^k$, is designated $_t r_{n-k,t+k}$ and called the forward rate at period t for an $(n - k)$-period forward investment commencing in period $t + k$. The first subscript refers, then, to the market date on which the rate is established (taken to be the beginning of period t), the second to the duration of the investment, and the third to the period at the beginning of which the forward loan commences. When the second

PRELIMINARIES 7

subscript is omitted, a one-period forward rate will be understood. The forward rate satisfies the relation

$$(1 + R_{k,t})^k = \frac{(1 + R_{n,t})^n}{(1 + {}_t r_{n-k,t+k})^{n-k}},\qquad(2.3)$$

or, solving for the forward rate,

$${}_t r_{n-k,t+k} = \left[\frac{(1 + R_{n,t})^n}{(1 + R_{k,t})^k}\right]^{1/(n-k)} - 1.\qquad(2.4)$$

Using this general relationship we see that the rate of return
for the example of a ten-period forward loan to begin ten
periods in the future is

$${}_t r_{10,t+10} = \left[\frac{(1 + R_{20,t})^{20}}{(1 + R_{10,t})^{10}}\right]^{1/10}.\qquad(2.5)$$

Clearly an $(n - k)$-period forward borrowing may be ar-
ranged to begin k periods ahead by buying a k-period bond
and selling an n-period bond. The forward rate on such a
forward borrowing will be given by (2.4) since it is the rate
that discounts the end payment, $(1 + R_{n,t})^n$, to the amount
of the forward borrowing, $(1 + R_{k,t})^k$.

The sequence of one-period forward rates, ${}_t r_{t+i}$, may be
built up from the spot rates, $R_{i,t}$, using the relationship (2.4),
which gives

$${}_t r_{t+i} = \frac{(1 + R_{i+1,t})^{i+1}}{(1 + R_{i,t})^i} - 1.\qquad(2.6)$$

Recognizing that ${}_t r_t = R_{1,t}$ and applying (2.6) recursively we
have

$$\begin{aligned}1 + R_{1,t} &= 1 + {}_t r_t,\\1 + R_{2,t} &= [(1 + {}_t r_t)(1 + {}_t r_{t+1})]^{1/2},\\&\;\;\vdots\\1 + R_{i,t} &= [(1 + {}_t r_t) \cdots (1 + {}_t r_{t+i-1})]^{1/i}.\end{aligned}\qquad(2.7)$$

The spot rates, then, are related to the long-term rate by a geometric average. Thus, montonically rising forward rates imply a rising yield curve and falling forward rates a falling yield curve.

Forward rates for a given future interval are uniquely determined by the term structure. Consider two alternative ways of obtaining a forward investment to begin in period $t + k$ and end at the end of period $t + n - 1$. First one might sell a k-period bond and buy an n-period bond. Second, one might arrange two separate forward investments, one to commence at the beginning of period $t + k$ to run through period $t + m - 1$ and the next to commence at period $t + m$ and run through period $t + n - 1$, choosing m between k and n. The forward rate on the first (single-investment) scheme is just

$$1 + {}_tr_{n-k,t+k} = \left[\frac{(1 + R_{n,t})^n}{(1 + R_{k,t})^k} \right]^{1/(n-k)}. \tag{2.8}$$

The forward rate for the first investment in the second (two-investment) scheme is just

$$1 + {}_tr_{m-k,t+k} = \left[\frac{(1 + R_{m,t})^m}{(1 + R_{k,t})^k} \right]^{1/(m-k)}, \tag{2.9}$$

and for the second investment it is

$$1 + {}_tr_{n-m,t+m} = \left[\frac{(1 + R_{n,t})^n}{(1 + R_{m,t})^m} \right]^{1/(n-m)}. \tag{2.10}$$

Now the single forward rate that would yield the same average overall rate of return for the period $n - k$ denoted ${}_t\mathbf{r}_{n-k,t+k}$ is

$$
\begin{aligned}
{}_t\mathbf{r}_{n-k,t+k} &= [(1 + {}_tr_{m-k,t+k})^{m-k}(1 + {}_tr_{n-m,t+m})^{n-m}]^{1/(n-k)} - 1 \\
&= \left[\frac{(1 + R_{m,t})^m(1 + R_{n,t})^n}{(1 + R_{k,t})^k(1 + R_{m,t})^m} \right]^{1/(n-k)} - 1 \\
&= \left[\frac{(1 + R_{n,t})^n}{(1 + R_{k,t})^k} \right]^{1/(n-k)} - 1 \\
&= {}_tr_{n-k,t+k}.
\end{aligned}
\tag{2.11}
$$

Thus forward rates are unique.

It may be well to emphasize at this point that while forward rates as defined above may always be computed from observed long-term yields, they do not *simply by definition* constitute a rate at which forward transactions are made. They have economic content only if the kinds of transactions implied by the derivation of forward rates are possible in the market. Clearly, many market participants are not able to borrow and lend in the same term structure of rates. However, the forward position of a portfolio-holder may be altered by shifting the maturity composition of bonds held. Rather than issuing bonds of a given maturity, one may simply sell them out of portfolio holdings. The last consideration may lend additional plausibility to the notion of forward transactions in loans taking place in the real world.

Studies of the term structure frequently deal explicitly with the determination of forward rates rather than long-term rates per se. However, from the set of relations (2.6) and (2.7) it is clear that a set of long-term yields implies a set of forward rates and vice versa. Thus we see that a theory of the determination of one implies the determination of the other.

DISCRETE LINEAR STOCHASTIC PROCESSES

Theories of the term structure of interest rates have generally assigned a central role to expectations of future spot rates in the determination of forward rates. Both for purposes of theoretical analysis and empirical testing we shall often find it useful to draw on the theory of discrete linear stochastic processes for additional insights into the role of expectations. The discussion that follows is intended to provide an introduction to discrete linear processes with implications for formation of expectations and adaptive revision of expectations by error learning.[6]

Consider a discrete time series, say Z_t, $Z_{t+1}, \ldots$, which may be regarded as a realization from a stochastic process, that is, a set of jointly distributed random variables indexed in time. That stochastic process is said to be linear if Z_t is generated by passing a sequence of independent and identically distributed disturbances with mean zero through a linear filter; that is,

$$Z_t = \mu + u_t + \psi_1 u_{t-1} + \psi_2 u_{t-2} + \cdots, \tag{2.12}$$

where the u_t are the white-noise disturbances and μ and the set of weights $\{\psi_i\}$ are fixed parameters. The process $\{Z_t\}$ is said to be stationary if the joint distribution for a realization of the process is invariant with respect to displacement on the time axis. If the series $(1 + \psi_1 B + \psi_2 B^2 + \cdots)$ converges for $|B| < 1$, that is, on or within the unit circle, then the mean, variance, and serial covariances of $\{Z_t\}$ exist (assuming the variance of u_t exists) and the process is stationary since all the moments are clearly invariant with respect to time. For the mean of Z_t we have

$$E(Z_t) = \mu; \tag{2.13}$$

for the variance,

$$V(Z_t) = (1 + \psi_1^2 + \psi_2^2 + \cdots)\,\sigma_u^2; \tag{2.14}$$

and for the serial covariances,

$$C(Z_t, Z_{t+k}) = (\psi_k + \psi_1\psi_{k+1} + \cdots)\sigma_u^2. \tag{2.15}$$

The behavior of a stationary process is characterized by a wandering about on either side of the mean and, if the state space is continuous, repeated returns to the neighborhood of the mean.

A notationally simpler and more convenient way of writing process (2.12) is in the form

$$Z_t = \mu + \psi(B)u_t, \tag{2.16}$$

where

$$\psi(B) = (1 + \psi_1 B + \psi_2 B^2 + \cdots) \tag{2.17}$$

in which B is the backshift operator; i.e., $B^k Z_t = Z_{t-k}$. Another form of the process is obtained by dividing (2.16) through $\psi(B)$, the result being written as

$$\pi(B)Z_t = \theta_0 + u_t, \tag{2.18}$$

where

$$\pi(B) = (1 - \pi_1 B - \pi_2 B^2 - \cdots) = [\psi(B)]^{-1} \tag{2.19}$$

and

$$\theta_0 = [\psi(1)]^{-1}\mu. \tag{2.20}$$

The weights π_i in $\pi(B)$ may in principle be computed by matching coefficients of B^i in the relation

$$\pi(B)\psi(B) = 1, \tag{2.21}$$

which follows from (2.19).

When $\pi_i = 0$ for $i > p$, the process is referred to as an autoregressive (AR) process of order p, denoted AR(p), and may be written as

$$\phi_p(B)Z_t = \theta_0 + u_t, \tag{2.22}$$

where

$$\phi_p(B) = (1 - \phi_1 B - \cdots - \phi_p B^p). \tag{2.23}$$

The condition required of $\phi_p(B)$ for stationarity is that its roots lie outside the unit circle. A simple and instructive example is the AR(1) process,

$$Z_t = \phi_1 Z_{t-1} + \theta_0 + u_t, \tag{2.24}$$

or equivalently,

$$Z_t = \frac{\theta_0}{1 - \phi_1} + u_t + \phi_1 u_{t-1} + \theta_1^2 u_{t-2} + \cdots. \qquad (2.25)$$

Stationarity requires that $|\phi| < 1$ in which case we have

$$E(Z_t) = \frac{\theta_0}{1 - \phi_1}, \qquad (2.26)$$

$$V(Z_t) = \frac{\sigma_u^2}{1 - \phi_1^2}, \qquad (2.27)$$

and

$$C(Z_t, Z_{t+k}) = \frac{\phi^k \sigma_u^2}{1 - \phi_1^2}. \qquad (2.28)$$

For ϕ_1 equal to unity, $\{Z_t\}$ is a random walk, the expected value of Z_t does not exist, and the process is nonstationary. For $|\phi_1|$ greater than unity, the process clearly behaves in an explosive manner, and, of course, is nonstationary.

When a linear process is written in the form (2.12) and the weights $\psi_i = 0$ for $i > q$, the process is said to be a moving-average (MA) process of order q and may be written as

$$Z_t = \theta_0 + \theta_q(B)u_t, \qquad (2.29)$$

where

$$\theta_q(B) = (1 - \theta_1 B - \cdots - \theta_q B^q). \qquad (2.30)$$

The fact that $\psi_i = 0$ for $i > q$ ensures stationarity. The mean, variance, and serial covariances of $\{Z_t\}$ are given by (2.13), (2.14), and (2.15). In the case $q = 1$ these moments are

$$E(Z_t) = \theta_0, \qquad (2.31)$$
$$V(Z_t) = (1 + \theta_1^2)\sigma_u^2, \qquad (2.32)$$

and

$$C(Z_t, Z_{t+k}) = -\theta_1 \sigma_u^2. \qquad (2.33)$$

We note that process (2.29) with $q = 1$ may also be expressed as

$$Z_t = (-\theta_1 Z_{t-1} - \theta_1^2 Z_{t-2} - \cdots) + \frac{\theta_0}{\theta(1)} + u_t. \qquad (2.34)$$

If Z_t is not to depend increasingly on more distantly past Z_{t-k} in (2.34), we require that $|\theta_1| < 1$. This *invertibility* condition may be generalized to higher-order moving-average processes by requiring that the roots of $\theta_q(B)$ lie outside the unit circle.

Box and Jenkins have suggested that many processes encountered in practice may be economically represented by linear processes of mixed autoregressive–moving-average form; that is,

$$\phi_p(B)Z_t = \theta_0 + \theta_q(B)u_t, \qquad (2.35)$$

denoted ARMA(p,q). The $\psi(B)$ polynomial implied by the ARMA(p,q) polynomials is given by

$$\psi(B) = [\phi_p(B)]^{-1}\theta_q(B) \qquad (2.36)$$

and the ψ_i weights may be computed by matching coefficients of B^i in the relation

$$\phi_p(B)\psi(B) = \theta_q(B). \qquad (2.37)$$

Conditions for stationarity and invertibility are the same as those required for pure AR(p) and MA(q) processes.

To see how the ARMA(p,q) model achieves parsimony in paramaterization suppose that the process $\{Z_t\}$ were generated according to the ARMA(1,1) scheme

$$Z_t = \phi_1 Z_{t-1} + \theta_0 + u_t - \theta_1 u_{t-1}. \qquad (2.38)$$

If the process is expressed in pure autoregressive form, we have the AR(∞) process

$$Z_t = [(\phi_1 - \theta_1)Z_{t-1} + (\phi_1 - \theta_1)\theta_1 Z_{t-2}$$
$$+ (\phi_1 - \theta_1)\theta_1^2 Z_{t-2} + \cdots] + \frac{\theta_0}{1 - \theta_1} + u_t. \qquad (2.39)$$

Clearly, an attempt to relate Z_t to its past values in this way might require several terms before $(\phi_1 - \theta_1)\theta_1^k$ becomes small enough to neglect.

Certainly many economic time series appear to exhibit *nonstationary* behavior. It is difficult, for example, to think of the price of IBM stock as being stationary and having some mean value. Rather, that series seems to move freely and its local behavior appears to be independent of its level, that is, "homogeneous" in space. To account for such behavior within the framework of linear processes one might consider an autoregressive polynomial $\Phi_p(B)$ such that a change in the level of Z_t by amount c has no effect on the behavior of the process; that is,

$$\Phi_p(B)(Z_t + c) = \Phi_p(B)Z_t. \tag{2.40}$$

For (2.40) to hold, $\Phi_p(B)$ must be of the form

$$\Phi_p(B) = (1 - B)\phi_{p-1}(B); \tag{2.41}$$

that is, $\Phi_p(B)$ contains at least one difference operator $1 - B$. This leads us to consider a class of models for nonstationary series of the form

$$\phi_p(B)(1 - B)^d Z_t = \theta_0 + \theta_q(B)u_t, \tag{2.42}$$

which we shall refer to as integrated autoregressive–moving-average models of order p, d, and q or just ARIMA(p,d,q). The autoregressive and moving-average polynomials $\phi_p(B)$ and $\theta_q(B)$ satisfy stationarity and invertibility conditions and describe a stationary linear process in the dth difference of Z_t.

The parameters of the process that generates $\{Z_t\}$ imply a distribution for future Z_ts conditioned on the history of $\{Z_t\}$ up to the present. The mean of that distribution provides minimum mean-square-error forecasts. To show this we let $_tZ^*_{t+n}$ denote the expected value of Z_{t+n} conditional on $\ldots, Z_{t-1}, Z_t$ and let $_tF_{t+n}$ denote another forecast that differs from $_tZ^*_{t+n}$ by amount d. The mean square error for $_tF_{t+n}$ is

$$E(Z_{t+n} - {_tF_{t+n}}) = E(Z_{t+n} - {_tZ^*_{t+n}}) + d^2, \qquad (2.43)$$

which is minimized for $d = 0$; i.e., $_tF_{t+n} = {_tZ^*_{t+n}}$.

From Equation (2.18) for Z_t in terms of its past history the conditional expectation $_tZ^*_{t+1}$ is seen to be given in general by

$$_tZ^*_{t+1} = \pi_1 Z_t + \pi_2 Z_{t-1} + \cdots. \qquad (2.44)$$

From (2.18) and (2.44) the one-step-ahead forecast error associated with $_tZ^*_{t+1}$ is then

$$Z_{t+1} - {_tZ^*_{t+1}} = u_{t+1}, \qquad (2.45)$$

the disturbance occurring contemporaneously with Z_{t+1}. This result allows operational computation of conditional expectations to proceed directly from the ARMA form of the process as follows. The one-step-ahead conditional expectation $_tZ^*_{t+1}$ is

$$\begin{aligned}_tZ^*_{t+1} = {}&\phi_1 Z_t + \cdots + \phi_p Z_{t-p+1} + \theta_0 \\ &- \theta_1 u_t - \cdots - \theta_q u_{t-q+1}\end{aligned} \qquad (2.46)$$

in which the "unobserved" u_{t-k} are provided by past forecast errors $Z_{t-k} - {_{t-k-1}Z^*_{t-k}}$. The two-step-ahead conditional expectation $_tZ^*_{t+2}$ is then

$$\begin{aligned}_tZ^*_{t+2} = {}&\phi_{1t}Z^*_{t+1} + \phi_2 Z_t + \cdots + \phi_p Z_{t-p+2} + \theta_0 \\ &- \theta_2 u_t - \cdots - \theta_q u_{t-q+2}.\end{aligned} \qquad (2.47)$$

From (2.46) and (2.47) it is clear that conditional expectations for successively longer horizons may be computed recursively using initial conditions drawn from the past history of $\{Z_t\}$ and from past forecast errors.

The rule for revision of conditional expectations by error learning is easily derived from (2.12), which implies that

$$_tZ^*_{t+n} = \mu + \psi_n u_t + \psi_{n+1} u_{t-1} + \cdots \qquad (2.48)$$

and that in the previous period the corresponding conditional expectation was

$$_{t-1}Z^*_{t+n} = \mu + \psi_{n+1} u_{t-1} + \psi_{n+2} u_{t-2} + \cdots. \qquad (2.49)$$

Consequently, the revision of conditional expectations is given by

$$_tZ^*_{t+n} - _{t-1}Z^*_{t+n} = \psi_n u_t \qquad (2.50)$$

or, in view of (2.46), by

$$_tZ^*_{t+n} - _{t-1}Z^*_{t+n} = \psi_n(Z_t - _{t-1}Z^*_t). \qquad (2.51)$$

Thus the change in the conditional expectation for horizon n periods in response to the current forecast error is determined by the coefficient of u_{t-n} in the pure moving-average representation of the process.

These general results are called upon for application in the following chapters. The problem of identifying a process appropriate to a set of observed data and estimation of parameters will be discussed in Chapter 5, where results for the sequence of one-year yields in the Durand data are presented.

Notes

1. Neil Wallace, "The Term Structure of Interest Rates and the Maturity Composition of the Federal Debt" (unpublished Ph.D. dissertation, University of Chicago, 1964), pp. 10–12.
2. Burton G. Malkiel, *The Term Structure of Interest Rates: Expectations and Behavior Patterns* (Princeton, N.J.: Princeton University Press, 1966), pp. 40–49.

3. Sources for the Durand yield-curve series: 1900–1942—David Durand, *Basic Yields of Corporate Bonds, 1900–1942,* Technical Paper 3 (New York: National Bureau of Economic Research, 1942); 1943–1947—David Durand and Willis J. Winn, *Basic Yields of Bonds, 1926–1947: Their Management and Pattern,* Technical Paper 6 (New York: National Bureau of Economic Research, 1947); 1948–1952—*The Economic Almanac, 1953–1954* (New York: National Industrial Conference Board, 1953); 1953–1958—David Durand, "A Quarterly Series of Corporate Basic Yields, 1952–1957, and Some Attendant Reservations," *The Journal of Finance* 13 (September 1958): 3–5.

4. Yield curves for U.S. Treasury securities appear in the monthly periodical *Treasury Bulletin* (Washington, D.C.: U.S. Treasury Department).

5. For discussion of these problems, see David Meiselman, *The Term Structure of Interest Rates* (Englewood Cliffs, N.J.: Prentice-Hall, Inc., 1962), p. 63; and James Van Horne, "Interest Rate Risk and the Term Structure of Interest Rates," *Journal of Political Economy* 73 (August 1965): 350–351.

6. For a more detailed treatment of the topics discussed in this section the reader is referred to G. E. P. Box and G. M. Jenkins, *Time Series Analysis for Forecasting and Control* (San Francisco: Holden-Day, Inc., 1970), upon which I have drawn for this discussion.

Theories of the Term Structure of Interest Rates and the Methodology of Empirical Tests

TRADITIONAL EXPECTATIONS THEORY

A spot market in bonds of varying maturities implies, as we have seen in Chapter 2, the existence of a futures market in bonds. This statement is simply the result of algebraic relationships and is not a statement of behavior. However, if participants hold expectations of future rates and seek to maximize expected profits, then they may make use of the forward aspects of the market in order to be short or long on loans depending on whether they expect future spot rates to be higher or lower than current forward rates. As a matter of actual practice, the participant may simply shift the maturity composition of his portfolio according to his expectations. The general proposition that expectations influence long-term rates through the forward-rate structure is referred to in the literature as the *expectations theory*. The *traditional expectations theory* abstracts from real-world considerations such as tax features, transaction costs, and uncertainty, so that expectations of future short rates are held uniformly by participants and are viewed as certainties. Then as participants seek to maximize return over their particular holding period, they will drive forward rates to the level of future short-term rates. This result follows from the fact that securities will be purchased or sold in the sequence that will maximize return over some holding period. Hence, for example, if one- and two-period bonds are traded and a lender's holding period is two periods, he may buy a two-period bond or two one-period bonds sequentially. So if the forward rate for the second period is less than his expectation of what the one-period rate will be one period hence, he has the option of lending for this period and then waiting to lend for the second period at the higher one-period rate that he expects (with complete certainty) to materialize. In equilibrium, then, forward rates will be equal to expected short rates. An important implication of the traditional expectations theory is that realized rates of return for bonds of different maturities over a given holding period will be the same.[1]

Early tests of the traditional theory focused on the evaluation of forward rates as forecasts. Hickman compared forward rates with realized short-term rates for the period 1935–1942 and found that an inertia hypothesis, i.e., that $R_{1,t} = R_{1,t+1}$, yielded better forecasts than did forward rates.[2] Macaulay found that 90-day money rates moved in anticipation of the seasonal fluctuation in call-money rates but otherwise found no evidence of successful forecasting.[3] More recently Culbertson tested the implication of the traditional expectations hypothesis that realized returns on holding bonds of different maturities should be equal.[4] He examined one- and three-week holding-period returns for bills and long-term Treasury bonds, found they were not equal, and hence rejected the expectations hypothesis.

LIQUIDITY PREFERENCE THEORY

The traditional theory may be extended by relaxing the certainty assumption and replacing it with the assumption that market participants form expectations of uncertain future spot rates. Hicks proposed the *liquidity preference theory*, suggesting that borrowing is typically undertaken to finance long-term projects and that such borrowers prefer to issue long-term securities so as to hedge against the risk of fluctuations in interest cost.[5] Lenders, according to the theory, prefer to hold short-term securities to avoid the fluctuations in portfolio value associated with holding long-term securities. Note that hedging behavior arises owing to risk aversion, the preference for a less risky return of given expected value over a more risky one of the same expected value. While *risk* may be identified in this context with variance of return, other characteristics of the distribution of returns, such as skewness, might well enter into the preference orderings of participants.[6]

The assumptions of the liquidity preference theory imply that lenders must be paid a *liquidity premium* over expected future short-term rates and that this premium rises monotonically with term. Denoting the expected value in period t of the future short-term rate R_{t+k} as $_tR^*_{t+k}$ for a distribution of future short-term rates held uniformly by participants, the theory implies that

$$_tr_{t+k} = {_tR^*_{t+k}} + L_k \qquad (3.1)$$

and that

$$0 < L_1 < L_2 < \cdots < L_k < \cdots, \qquad (3.2)$$

where L_k is the liquidity premium associated with the k-period-ahead forward rate. The liquidity premiums are invariant with time since they represent a "normal backwardation" of the forward market. Note that the Hicks model depends on a particular distribution of preferred holding periods. If borrowers had a strong preference for short-term borrowing, while lenders preferred predominantly long holding periods, then borrowers would presumably have to pay lenders a premium for short-term money since the lenders would thereby expose themselves to uncertainty of income level. There are, in fact, several types of lenders with long holding periods, for example, insurance companies and pension trusts. Thus there seem to be no a priori grounds on which to accept the term shape of the Hicksian liquidity premium.

Evidence for the Liquidity Preference Theory from Average Differentials Between Short- and Long-term Interest Rates.

Long-term interest rates have indeed been higher on average than short-term rates during the twentieth century, as the liquidity preference theory would predict. The average differential over the period 1900–1958 between long-term interest rates and spot one-year rates in the Durand yield-curve data increases monotonically with term to about half a percentage point at forty years. The interpretation given to these differentials in the term-structure literature is that they are the additional rate of return earned on average by capital invested in long-term bonds and, thus, constitute evidence favorable to the liquidity preference theory.[7]

An average differential between long- and short-term interest rates, however, does not necessarily represent a differential between realized rates of return, because the realized increment to capital invested in a sequence of short-term bonds depends on the ex post product of uncertain future spot rates. The expected value of this ex post product will in general differ from the product of expected future spot rates. If short-term rates are positively autocorrelated, then interest-rate differentials overstate differentials in realized rates of return.

To compare the rates of return that result from investing in a long-term bond as opposed to a sequence of one-period bonds we begin by comparing the increment to capital offered by a two period and a two-period succession of one-period bonds.

If the rate of interest on two-period bonds at market date t is $R_{2,t}$, then the associated two-period increment is $(1 + R_{2,t})^2$. The increment resulting from a two-period sequence of one-period bonds is correspondingly $(1 + R_{1,t})(1 + R_{1,t+1})$ in which the one-period rate one period hence is a random variable and, hence, so is the increment. The expected value of this random increment at time t is just $(1 + R_{1,t})[1 + E_t(R_{1,t+1})]$, where E_t denotes expected value over the distribution of future spot rates conditional on information available at time t. Now the two-period bond increment can be decomposed as $(1 + R_{1,t})(1 + {}_t r_{1,t+1})$, where, in general, ${}_t r_{k,t+n}$ denotes the k-period forward rate n periods hence as implied by the term structure at t. Clearly, if the forward rate ${}_t r_{1,t+1}$ is given by

$$_t r_{1,t+1} = E_t(R_{1,t+1}), \tag{3.3}$$

then the two increments and thus rates of return are equal. If this equality were to hold, then over a long history of interest rates the average of one-period-ahead forward rates would be approximately equal to the average of one-period spot rates.

Now consider the same comparison for three-period bonds and a three-period succession of one-period bonds. The increment offered by the three-period bond is $(1 + R_{3,t})^3$, which may be decomposed as $(1 + R_{1,t})(1 + {}_tr_{1,t+1})(1 + {}_tr_{1,t+2})$. The ex post increment resulting from the three-period succession of one-period bonds is $(1 + R_{1,t})(1 + R_{1,t+1})(1 + R_{1,t+2})$, which is a random variable at time t. This random increment has expected value

$$E_t(1 + R_{1,t})(1 + R_{1,t+1})(1 + R_{1,t+2}) = (1 + R_{1,t})[1 + E_t(R_{1,t+1}) \\ + E_t(R_{1,t+2}) + E_t(R_{1,t+1}R_{1,t+2})]. \quad (3.4)$$

Suppose for the moment that the two forward rates ${}_tr_{1,t+1}$ and ${}_tr_{1,t+2}$ are just equal to the expected values of corresponding future spot rates. In that case we may express the three-period bond increment as

$$(1 + R_{3,t})^3 = (1 + R_{1,t})[1 + E_t(R_{1,t+1}) + E_t(R_{1,t+2}) \\ + E_t(R_{1,t+1})E_t(R_{1,t+2})]. \quad (3.5)$$

The difference between ex ante increments (3.4) and (3.5) is

$$E_t(R_{1,t+1}R_{1,t+2}) - E_t(R_{1,t+1})E_t(R_{1,t+2}) = \text{Cov}_t(R_{1,t+1},R_{1,t+2}), \quad (3.6)$$

where $\text{Cov}_t(\ )$ denotes the covariance over the conditional joint distribution of future one-period spot rates at time t. If spot rates are positively autocorrelated, $\text{Cov}_t(\ )$ will be positive and the ex ante expected increment offered by a sequence of one-period bonds is higher than the three-period bond increment.

The ex ante increments would be equal if the covariance term were added to the three-period bond increment. Assuming that two-period increments have been equalized by setting ${}_tr_{1,t+1}$ equal to $E_t(R_{1,t+1})$, the equivalence of three-period increments implies

$$_tr_{1,t+2} = E_t(R_{1,t+2}) + \frac{\text{Cov}_t(R_{1,t+1},R_{1,t+2})}{1 + {}_tr_{1,t+1}}, \quad (3.7)$$

namely that the two-period-ahead forward rate will exceed the corresponding expected future spot rate. Thus if holders of three-period bonds just realize the same average rate of return as do holders of successive one-period bonds, it must be that there will be a positive average differential between two-period-ahead forward rates (and thus three-period rates) and one-period rates.

It is interesting at this point to consider an intuitive explanation of why the ex ante expected increment from successive one-period bonds exceeds the increment offered by long-term bonds in which forward rates are equal to corresponding expected future spot rates. If one-period rates are positively autocorrelated, when the realized value of $R_{1,t+1}$ is above its mean, $R_{1,t+2}$, $R_{1,t+3}$, etc., will tend to be above their means also. Similarly, if $R_{1,t+1}$ is below its mean, subsequent one-period rates will tend to be below their means. The additional increment that accrues in the case of successive realized rates being above their means more than offsets the reduction that results from being below. We might expect that this effect of serial correlation would increase with the length of the sequence, but tend to a limit as realized values became distributed around their expected values. This intuitive judgment will be confirmed by evaluation of that limit.

To facilitate our further analysis, we shall assume that investors make their computations in terms of continuous interest rates. Thus the increment offered by a n-period bond is $\exp(nR_{n,t})$. The corresponding increment resulting from a sequence of one-period bonds is $\exp(R_{1,t} + \cdots + R_{1,t+n-1})$. If the sequence of one-period rates is a normal stochastic process, then increments on future rates have a log-normal distribution.[8]

The expected value at time t of the increment for one-period bonds is

$$E_t[\exp(R_{1,t} + \cdots + R_{1,t+n-1})] = \exp[(R_{1,t} + \cdots + E_t(R_{1,t+n-1})$$
$$+ \tfrac{1}{2}V_t(R_{1,t+1} + \cdots + R_{1,t+n-1})], \quad (3.8)$$

where $V_t(\ )$ denotes variance over the conditional distribution of future rates at time t. If the long-term rate $R_{n,t}$ embodies a liquidity premium, in the sense of offering a larger increment than the sequence of one-period bonds, then that premium, denoted L'_n, will satisfy the equality

$$\exp(nR_{n,t}) = \exp\left[R_{1,t} + \cdots + E_t(R_{1,t+n-1}) + \frac{1}{2}\sum_{i=1}^{n-1}\sum_{j=1}^{n-1} C_{ij}\right]$$
$$\times \exp(nL'_n) \quad (3.9)$$

in which the variance of the sum of future rates is expressed as the sum of conditional variances, denoted C_{ii}, and covariances, denoted C_{ij}, associated with pairs (R_{t+i}, R_{t+j}).

Taking logs in (3.9) we obtain the long-term rate as

$$R_{n,t} = \frac{1}{n}[R_{1,t} + \cdots + E_t(R_{1,t+n-1})] + A'_n + L'_n, \quad (3.10)$$

where

$$A'_n = \frac{1}{n}\left(\frac{1}{2}\sum_{i=1}^{n-1}\sum_{j=1}^{n-1} C_{ij}\right). \quad (3.11)$$

Over a long history of interest rates the average of conditional expectations on the right-hand side of (3.10) would be approximately equal to the average of one-period rates. Thus (3.10) implies the approximate equality

$$\bar{R}_n \doteq \bar{R}_1 + A'_n + L'_n \quad (3.12)$$

or

$$L'_n \doteq (\bar{R}_n - \bar{R}_1) - A'_n, \quad (3.13)$$

where overbars denote averages. We see that a positive average differential between long-term and one-period bonds, as in the Durand data, cannot be attributed exclusively to the premium L'_n. Rather, since the adjustment factor A'_n is a variance and therefore positive, the premium is something less than the differential and could perfectly well be negative.

The relation of forward rates to the expected future spot rates is easily obtained from (3.10) as

$$_t r_{1,t+n} = (n+1)R_{n+1,t} - (n)R_{n,t} = E_t(R_{1,t+n}) + A_n + L_n, \quad (3.14)$$

where

$$A_n = (n+1)A'_{n+1} - nA'_n = \frac{1}{2}\left(C_{nn} + 2\sum_{i=1}^{n-1} C_{ni}\right), \quad (3.15)$$

and

$$L_n = (n+1)L'_{n+1} - (n)L'_n \quad (3.16)$$

is the premium embodied in forward rates. If we again consider a long history of yield curves, there will be the approximate equality

$$\bar{r}_n \doteq \bar{R}_1 + A_n + L_n \quad (3.17)$$

or

$$L_n \doteq (\bar{r}_n - \bar{R}_1) - A_n. \quad (3.18)$$

We must conclude, then, that a positive average differential between forward and one-period rates cannot be identified with the liquidity premium L_n.

To evaluate the conditional variances and covariances appearing in adjustment factors A'_n and A_n we must specify the form of the normal stochastic process generating one-period rates. We shall assume that that process is a discrete linear and stationary process of the form (2.12).

Computation of adjustment factors A'_n and A_n requires conditional variances and covariances, which are easily obtained from (2.14) and (2.15) as

$$C_{nn} = \sigma_u^2 \sum_{j=0}^{n-1} \psi_j^2 \quad (3.19)$$

and

$$C_{ni} = \sigma_u^2 \sum_{j=0}^{i-1} \psi_j \psi_{j+n-i}. \tag{3.20}$$

We indicated earlier that intuition would lead us to suspect that adjustment factors A_n' and A_n reach a limit as n gets large. Those limits may be evaluated with the help of the covariance generating function, which we defined as

$$K(B) = \sum_{i=-\infty}^{\infty} K_{ni} B^{n-i} = K_{nn} + 2 \sum_{i=-\infty}^{n-1} K_{ni} B^{n-i}, \tag{3.21}$$

where K_{ni} is the covariance between $R_{1,t+i}$ and $R_{1,t+n}$ over their joint distribution defined by process (2.12). It can be shown that for such a process $K(B)$ is given by

$$K(B) = \sigma_u^2 \frac{\theta_q(B)\theta_q(B^{-1})}{\phi_p(B)\phi_p(B^{-1})}. \tag{3.22}$$

Using the definition of K_{ni} and expressions (3.19) and (3.20) we let $i = n - k$ and obtain

$$\lim_{n\to\infty} C_{n,n-k} = K_{n,n-k} \tag{3.23}$$

and

$$\lim_{n\to\infty} C_{nn} = K_{nn}. \tag{3.24}$$

Hence, from (3.21)—the definition of A_n given by (3.11)—and (3.22), it follows that

$$\lim_{n\to\infty} A_n = \frac{1}{2} K(1) = \frac{1}{2} \sigma_u^2 \frac{\theta_q^2(1)}{\phi_p^2(1)}, \tag{3.25}$$

which provides the limit of A_n given the parameters of process (2.12). The limit of A_n' is easily shown to be the same as that of A_n.

To obtain a numerical estimate of these adjustment factors and, thus, assess the evidence available from the Durand data we utilize a result from Chapter 5, where it is shown that the one-year yields are reasonably represented by the linear process

$$R_{1,t} = .7987R_{1,t-1} + .1338R_{1,t-2} + .002237 \qquad (3.26)$$
$$\sigma_u^2 = .000047.$$

Using these estimated parameter values relation (3.25) provides

$$\frac{1}{2}\sigma_u^2 \frac{\theta_0^2(1)}{\phi_2^2(1)} = .0052, \qquad (3.27)$$

or .52 percentage points as an estimate of the limit of the adjustment factors. The average forward-rate curve for the Durand data is essentially flat for horizons of eight years and longer, so that the average differential between forward rates of those maturities and one-year spot yields may be taken as approximately the limiting differential. That differential is .49 percentage points, which may be entirely accounted for by the estimated adjustment factor.

In general, then, average-yield or forward-rate differentials per se do not constitute evidence of the existence of liquidity premiums. The average forward-rate differential observed in the Durand data at long horizons may simply be due, as we have shown, to the effect of autocorrelation in one-year yields and, thus, cannot be regarded as evidence in support of the liquidity preference theory.

PREFERRED HABITAT THEORY

A more recent theoretical structure that generalizes the assumption of the liquidity preference theory is the *preferred habitat theory* of Modigliani and Sutch.[9] Participants on both sides of the market are assumed to have a range of maturities in which they prefer to operate but will move outside usual bounds if a sufficient rate differential is present. These preferred maturity ranges, or habitats, are assumed to overlap so that there is a continuum of excess demands for funds along the term axis. Modigliani and Sutch conclude, then, that a term premium structure, if present, will be a smooth function of term, but not necessarily monotonic. Further, the premium structure presumably shifts through time with the distribution of preferred habitats. According to the theory, a major change in the composition of Treasury obligations, such as that which occurred during Operation Twist, should have observable effects on the term structure.

In trying to test the theory, Modigliani and Sutch are confronted with the central methodological problem of empirical work in the term-structure area, namely the separation of the unobserved expectation component of forward rates from the term-premium component. The approach taken by Modigliani and Sutch was the ad hoc specification of an expectations mechanism in terms of current and lagged spot yields, a procedure common in econometric work generally. In particular, quarterly observations on U.S. Treasury bond yields were regressed on the current and sixteen-lagged bill yields using the Almon technique. The weighted average of bill yields was interpreted as the expectation component of bond yields and the high R^2 obtained as evidence of success in representing that component. When measures of the maturity composition of the federal debt were introduced as additional variables, in accordance with the implications of the preferred habitat theory, they contributed little to the explanatory power of the regressions.

The authors do not offer independent evidence of the forecasting power of the weighted average of bill yields to support their interpretation of it as the expectation component. In his thesis, however, Sutch also fits the weighted average as a forecasting function (extended to eighteen past quarters) to the one-quarter-ahead bill yield as a "final check on the reasonableness of the empirical model."[10] The weights obtained in the forecasting regression were very different from those obtained when the long-term bond yield was the dependent variable. The sum of the weights was small and not significant. Moreover, the residuals, which are one-step-ahead forecast errors, were serially correlated, indicating that the forecasting model was suboptimal in that it omitted information contained in past errors. Thus the expectation role imputed to the weighted average of bill yields was not supported by its performance as a forecasting function.

Information may be lost in a procedure of the kind used by Modigliani and Sutch if variables affecting term premiums are correlated with the bill yields composing the weighted average. It is difficult to imagine, for example, how an effect of the level of interest rates on term premiums might be empirically separated from the expectation component without prior identification of an appropriate forecasting function.

HEDGING PRESSURE THEORY

Taking the idea of preferred maturity ranges one step farther, Culbertson and others have suggested the *hedging pressure* or *institutional theory,* which states that very strong hedging motives in the market overwhelm very weak speculative forces.[11] Hence the term structure will depend mainly on the distribution of holding periods on each side of the market. Excess demands in different maturity ranges will depend on net hedging pressure, and the equilibrium rate structure is the combination of rates that reduces these excess demands to zero. Changes, then, in the supply or demand for debt of various maturities should be reflected in changes in the term structure.

MEISELMAN'S ERROR-LEARNING MODEL

Meiselman has suggested that the expectation theory can be reconciled with uncertainty and risk aversion since "individual transactors may still speculate or hedge on the basis of risk aversion, but the speculators who are indifferent to uncertainty will bulk sufficiently large to determine market rates on the basis of mathematical expectations alone."[12] Thus, risk-indifferent speculators will succeed in driving forward rates to the level of corresponding expected future spot rates. Previous tests of the expectations theory based on the accuracy of forward rates as forecasts were inappropriate, according to Meiselman, since the theory merely predicts that participants forecast, not necessarily that their forecasts are accurate. Direct observation of expectations, however, is difficult if not conceptually impossible. These considerations led Meiselman to seek indirect evidence for the expectations theory in the behavior of forward rates themselves.

In suggesting his error-learning model, Meiselman noted the empirical successes in other areas of economics of hypotheses that relate expectations to past experience and that imply that *changes* in expectations are related to *unanticipated* events. The functional manifestation given by Meiselman to this idea in terms of the behavior of forward rates is a set of equations of the form

$$_t r_{t+n} - \,_{t-1}r_{t+n} = \alpha_n + \beta_n(R_{1,t} - \,_{t-1}r_t), \qquad n = 1, 2, \ldots . \quad (3.28)$$

The equations state that the revision at time t of the forward rate pertaining to period $t + n$, what is "learned," is linearly related to the current "error" made by the forward rate in forecasting the spot rate. If forward rates are expected rates, then the forward-rate error must indeed be unanticipated and, thus, trigger the revision of expectations. This general framework provides no a priori information on appropriate magnitudes for the revision coefficients, β_n, or about any sequential relationship between them.

The expectations theory, however, does imply that the constant terms, α_n, are zero, since there must be no systematic (predictable) trend in forward rates as a function of horizon. Inclusion of the constant terms in estimating the parameters of (3.28) allows the model to accommodate the possibility that forward rates are not just expected future spot rates but are additively biased forecasts. That is, if forward rates consist of the expected future spot rate plus a liquidity premium, then forward rates may be revised even when the forward-rate error is zero.

Meiselman estimated the parameters of (3.28) by ordinary least squares for $n = 1, \ldots, 8$ years using the Durand annual yield-curve data over the period 1901–1954.[13] The estimates of the β_n were highly significant and, thus, consistent with the hypothesized role of forward rates as expected rates. However, this is a very weak test of the expectations theory because the theory per se simply predicts correlation between revisions and errors, but, as we have noted, nothing about the magnitudes or relationship of the revision coefficients. More stringent criteria can be applied, as we shall see in Chapter 7, when properties of expectations appropriate to the stochastic structure of the sequence $\{R_{1,t}\}$ have been established.

The estimated constant terms α_n were all indistinguishable from zero, a fact that, as Meiselman pointed out, is consistent with the nonexistence of liquidity premiums.[14] It is also consistent, however, with the existence of liquidity premiums under special circumstances, as Kessel and Wood have pointed out.[15] If expected rates are revised according to an error-learning rule, then we have

$$_tR^*_{t+n} - {}_{t-1}R^*_{t+n} = \beta_n(R_{1,t} - {}_{t-1}R^*_t), \qquad (3.29)$$

which together with (3.1) implies that forward rates are revised according to

$$_tr_{t+n} - {}_{t-1}r_{t+n} = (L_n - L_{n+1} + \beta_nL_1) + \beta_n(R_{1,t} - {}_{t-1}r_t). \qquad (3.30)$$

Consequently, for the constant term to be zero it is sufficient that the liquidity premiums follow the relationships

$$L_{n+1} = L_n + \beta_nL_1. \qquad (3.31)$$

Thus the evidence presented by Meiselman cannot be construed as necessarily unfavorable to Hicks' hypothesis.

CYCLICAL MOVEMENT OF LIQUIDITY PREMIUMS

Within the framework of the liquidity preference theory, Kessel and Van Horne have suggested that liquidity premiums move cyclically with the general level of interest rates, but disagree on the direction of the effect.[16] Kessel argues that securities can be thought of as providing both a monetary yield and services as a money substitute. The yield differential between shorter- and longer-term securities reflects their relative value as money substitutes. An increase in interest rates raises the opportunity cost of holding money and therefore of money substitutes. Since short-term securities are better substitutes for money than long-term securities, Kessel argues, a rise in interest rates should imply a greater increase in the opportunity costs of holding the former than of holding the latter. Hence the spread must widen at higher levels of interest rates.

The evidence that Kessel presents in support of this hypothesis is based on regressions of the discrepancies between forward rates and subsequent spot rates on current spot rates. These discrepancies may rise because of the presence of liquidity premiums as well as because of errors in market expectations. Thus Kessel's hypothesis would imply positive slope coefficients. The Treasury yields used were at the very short end of the maturity spectrum, namely 28-day rates with forward rates computed 28 days ahead, and 91-day rates with forward rates 91 days ahead. For both maturities, it was found that in the regression

$$_t r_{1,t+1} - R_{1,t+1} = a + b R_{1,t} + e_t \qquad (3.32)$$

b was positive and significant. These results suggest that yield curves should be steepest at high interest-rate levels and flattest at low levels. As Kessel himself points out, this is true for the short end of the U.S. Treasury bill yield curve that he has considered, but not for the yield curve extending to long-term rates.[17] Hence we may entertain the possibility that his relationship will not hold for term premiums at longer maturities. In fact, if substitutability for cash is the source of the cyclical fluctuations in term premiums for short-term rates, we should not be surprised if we find that this factor is less important for longer maturities. This would account for the humping of the yield curve for Treasury securities that occurs at high interest levels in the short maturity range.

Van Horne has suggested that liquidity premiums vary inversely with the level of interest rates owing to corresponding variation in "interest rate risk."[18] Estimating the coefficients of Meiselman's error-learning model using monthly yield-curve data (September 1963–1964) for U.S. Treasury bonds Van Horne found that constant terms were positive and significant, which he interpreted as evidence of the presence of liquidity premiums.

In support of his hypothesis of interest-rate risk, Van Horne noted that *within clusters* of residuals from the Meiselman model there was a negative relationship between the residuals and the lagged forward rate $_{t-1}r_{t+n}$. These clusters were associated with different subperiods covered by the study. This analysis led to the introduction of the deviation of $_{t-1}r_{t+n}$ from the mean of its particular cluster as an additional variable to account for variation in liquidity premiums. Van Horne's version of the error-learning model then became

$$_{t}r_{t+n} - _{t-1}r_{t+n} = \alpha_n + \beta_n(R_{1,t} - _{t-1}r_t) + \gamma_n I_{n,t}, \qquad (3.33)$$

where $I_{n,t}$ was the interest-rate risk variable appropriate to horizon n. Van Horne's estimates of γ_n became increasingly negative and more significant with n.

It would appear, however, that Van Horne's model may be misspecified. Following his hypothesis that liquidity premiums vary linearly with $I_{n,t}$, forward rates are given by

$$_{t}r_{t+n} = _{t}R_{t+n}^* + (L_n + g_n I_{n,t}). \qquad (3.34)$$

Then if market expectations are revised according to an error-learning rule, forward rates are revised according to

$$(_{t}r_{t+n} - _{t-1}r_{t+n}) = \alpha_n + \beta_n(R_{1,t} - _{t-1}r_t) \\ + g_n I_{n,t} - g_{n+1}I_{n+1,t-1} + g_1\beta_n I_{1,t-1}, \qquad (3.35)$$

where α_n incorporates constant terms. Van Horne's regression

(3.33) omits variables $I_{n+1,t-1}$ and $I_{1,t-1}$, which, presumably, introduces bias into his estimate of g_n and, thus, the inferences that follow from it.

Nevertheless, it is clear that Van Horne generalized Meiselman's model in an important way. Namely he showed that the model could be extended to include determinants of fluctuations in liquidity premiums.

SUMMARY AND CONCLUSIONS

In this chapter we have tried to outline the main themes in the development of term-structure theory and the empirical methodologies that have accompanied them.

On the theoretical side, the most striking weakness is in the treatment of uncertainty. Hedging activities are suggested without explicit development of the basis for the demand and supply of hedges and, thus, of a model for the determination of forward rates.

On the empirical side, the central problem has been the devising of tests to detect the presence of expectational factors and to separate these from other components of forward rates. Early tests of the expectations theory focused on the accuracy of forward rates as forecasts as evidence for the role of expectations. More recently, Kessel examined forward-rate forecast errors for evidence of cyclical movement in liquidity premiums since systematic effects owing to expectations are presumably not present in the errors. Meiselman's error-learning model escaped the problem of measuring expectations by considering whether the response of formal rates to recent "errors" was *consistent* with the hypothesis that forward rates are expected rates. Van Horne showed that the systematic effect of nonexpectational factors could also be incorporated into the error-learning framework. Modigliani and Sutch attempted direct empirical estimation of the expectation component in order to detect the effect of changes in the maturity composition of the federal debt. What has been most conspicuously lacking in past empirical work has been a theoretical basis for the specification of the expectational models used and for the assessment of results.

The remaining chapters will deal with a model for the determination of forward rates that is developed by considering the maturity-choice problem facing a risk-averse market participant. The model is tested by utilizing implications of the theory of discrete linear stochastic processes for the formation and revision of expectations.

Notes

1. A more formal exposition of the traditional theory with further references is in Malkiel, *Term Structure of Interest Rates,* pp. 17–24.

2. William B. Hickman, *The Term Structure of Interest Rates: An Exploratory Analysis* (New York: National Bureau of Economic Research, 1943).

3. Frederick R. Macaulay, *The Movements of Interest Rates, Bond Yields, and Stock Prices in the United States Since 1856* (New York: National Bureau of Economic Research, 1938).

4. John M. Culbertson, "The Term Structure of Interest Rates," *Quarterly Journal of Economics* 71 (November 1957): 502.

5. John R. Hicks, *Value and Capital,* 2nd ed. (London: Clarendon Press, 1946), pp. 144–147.

6. For a rigorous discussion of the concept of risk aversion, the reader is referred to Kenneth J. Arrow, *Aspects of the Theory of Risk Bearing* (Helsinki: Yrjo Jahnsson Foundation, 1965), pp. 28–35.

7. For example, see Malkiel, *Term Structure of Interest Rates,* pp. 36–37; and Reuben A. Kessel, *The Cyclical Behavior of the Term Structure of Interest Rates* (New York: National Bureau of Economic Research, 1965), pp. 17–22. The interpretation introduced here is developed further in Charles R. Nelson, "Estimation of Term Premiums from Average Yield Differentials in the Term Structure of Interest Rates," forthcoming in *Econometrica.*

8. If x is normally distributed, then $\exp(x)$ has a log-normal distribution. The

expected value of exp(x) is exp[$E(x) + \frac{1}{2}V(x)$]. For a discussion of the log-normal distribution see J. A. Aitchison and J. A. C. Brown, *The Log-Normal Distribution* (Cambridge: Cambridge University Press, 1963).

9. Franco Modigliani and Richard Sutch, "Innovations in Interest Rate Policy," *American Economic Review* 56 (May 1966): 178–197; and Franco Modigliani and Richard Sutch, "Debt Management and the Term Structure of Interest Rates," *Journal of Political Economy* 75 (August 1967): 569–589.

10. Richard Sutch, "Expectations, Risk, and the Term Structure of Interest Rates" (unpublished Ph.D. dissertation, Massachusetts Institute of Technology, 1968), pp. 154–159, 384–386.

11. Culbertson, "Term Structure of Interest Rates," pp. 485–517.

12. Meiselman, *Term Structure of Interest Rates,* p. 10.

13. Meiselman, *Term Structure of Interest Rates,* p. 22.

14. *Ibid.,* pp. 44–47.

15. See Kessel, *Cyclical Behavior,* pp. 37ff.; and John H. Wood, "Expectations, Errors, and the Term Structure of Interest Rates," *The Journal of Political Economy* 71 (April 1963): p. 166.

16. Kessel, *Cyclical Behavior,* p. 25; and Van Horne, "Interest Rate Risk."

17. Kessel, *Cyclical Behavior,* p. 26.

18. Van Horne, "Interest Rate Risk," p. 347.

Model of the Cyclical
Movement of the Term
Structure of Interest Rates

INTRODUCTION

A long-term bond may be thought of as a tandem obligation consisting of a spot loan for the current period and forward-loan contracts for successive periods until the maturity date of the bond. Thus, for analytical purposes, a market in bonds of varying maturities may be conceptually dichotomized into a market in spot loans and a market in forward loans. The maturity-choice problem facing market participants then becomes one of choosing between forward commitments at forward rates established in the current period and future spot commitments at uncertain future spot rates.

The analysis of this problem that is presented in this chapter is based on maximization of the expected utility of real income by risk-averse market participants. Differentials between forward rates and expected future rates arise in the analysis from the conditions required for market equilibrium. We refer to these differentials as *term premiums* rather than liquidity premiums since their appearance in the model does not require an assumption of liquidity preference. The analysis suggests that term premiums vary inversely with the level of interest rates and with an indicator of business confidence.

FORWARD LOANS AND EXPECTED UTILITY

Consider a market in loans in which one-period loans for the current period are traded at a spot rate and one-period forward loans for the next period are traded at a forward rate. This is equivalent to saying that one- and two-period bonds are traded. Participants contracting to lend in the next period are said to have a long forward position, while those contracting to borrow take a short forward position. Each participant is assumed to anticipate either holding a portfolio of loans or having to borrow in the next period. We shall designate this anticipated spot position for the next period as W dollars, which is positive for portfolio holders and negative for borrowers. The forward position taken in the current period for loans in the next period is designated as F dollars, positive for long positions and negative for short. The real income (or loss) in the second period associated with a participant's position in the loan market is given by the sum of the amount earned (paid) on contracts obtained in the forward market of the previous period plus the amount earned (paid) on the remaining portion of W in the spot market of the second period. Designating this real income as y, the second-period spot rate as R, and the forward rate established in the first period as r and deflating forward and spot rates of return by the rate of change in prices, P, we have

$$y = F(r - P) + (W - F)(R - P) = F(r - R) + W(R - P)$$
$$= F(r - R) + Wi, \tag{4.1}$$

where i is used to designate the real interest rate. The last expression for y in (4.1) indicates that real income may be thought of as consisting of the extra amount earned as a result of having entered into forward contracts plus the amount that would have been earned anyway in spot investment of the portfolio.

If participants are uncertain in the first period about the values of R and P realized in the second period, then the realized value of y is uncertain and their decision problem is that of choosing F such that it maximizes the expected utility associated with y. We assume that a given participant has a subjective joint probability distribution for R and P, and hence for y, conditional on information available in the first period. Let his utility function on y be $U(y)$, having the properties that marginal utility of income, $U'(y)$, is positive but declines with y, so that $U''(y)$ is negative. We assume further that $U(y)$ is bounded and hence that the expected value of $U(y)$ is finite. These assumptions imply that $\lim_{y \to \infty} U''(y) = 0$, since $U(y)$ is monotonic. While $U''(y)$ need not necessarily rise monotonically with y toward zero, we shall assume that it does rise over a broad range, permitting us to assume that $U'''(y)$ is positive. We now have the following set of conditions:

$$U'(y) > 0, \tag{4.2}$$
$$U''(y) < 0, \tag{4.3}$$

and

$$U'''(y) > 0. \tag{4.4}$$

To obtain an expression for expected utility we first expand $U(y)$ in a Taylor series about y^*, the expected value of y, which gives us

$$U(y) = U(y^*) + U'(y^*)(y - y^*) + \tfrac{1}{2}U''(y^*)(y - y^*)^2$$
$$+ \tfrac{1}{6}U'''(y^*)(y - y^*)^3 + G, \qquad (4.5)$$

where G is a remainder in terms of higher powers of $y - y^*$. Taking the expectation of $U(y)$, denoted U^*, over the conditional distribution of y, we have from (4.5)

$$U^* = U(y^*) + \tfrac{1}{2}U''(y^*)\sigma_y^2 + \tfrac{1}{6}U'''(y^*)\sigma_y^3 + E(G), \qquad (4.6)$$

where σ_y^2 and σ_y^3 are the variance and third central moment of y, respectively, and $E(G)$ is the expectation of the remainder term consisting of terms in the fourth and higher central moments of y. If we assume for the time being that σ_y^3 and higher central moments are zero, then (4.6) reduces to

$$U^* = U(y^*) + \tfrac{1}{2}U''(y^*)\sigma_y^2. \qquad (4.7)$$

We see now that expected utility is a function of y^*, the expected value of y, and σ_y^2, the variance of y, permitting us to write U^* as

$$U^* = U^*(y^*, \sigma_y^2). \qquad (4.8)$$

If a person prefers the certain income y^* to the uncertain income y, he is said to be a risk-averter. For a risk-averter, then,

$$U(y^*) > U^*(y^*, \sigma_y^2), \qquad (4.9)$$

which together with (4.7) requires simply that

$$U''(y) < 0, \qquad (4.10)$$

which is condition (4.3). We note further that the partial derivative of expected utility with respect to y^* is

$$\frac{\partial U^*}{\partial y^*} = U'(y^*) + \frac{U'''(y^*)}{2}\sigma_y^2, \tag{4.11}$$

which from conditions (4.2) and (4.4) and the fact that $\sigma_y^2 \geq 0$ is clearly positive. Hence, for fixed σ_y^2, expected utility increases with y^*. The response of expected utility to increases in σ_y^2 is negative, since we have

$$\frac{\partial U^*}{\partial \sigma_y^2} = \frac{U''(y^*)}{2}. \tag{4.12}$$

We may think of indifference curves consisting of points (y^*, σ_y^2) yielding the same level of expected utility. For some fixed level of expected utility $\bar{U}^*$, these satisfy the implicit function

$$U(y^*) + \tfrac{1}{2}U''(y^*)\sigma_y^2 - \bar{U}^* = 0. \tag{4.13}$$

The slope of such an indifference curve is given by

$$\frac{\partial \sigma_y^2}{\partial y^*} = 2\left\{ \frac{U'''(y^*)[U(y^*) - \bar{U}^*]}{[U''(y^*)]^2} + \frac{-U'(y^*)}{U''(y^*)} \right\}. \tag{4.14}$$

This slope is positive since conditions (4.2) and (4.3) assure that the second term is positive and along with condition (4.9) that the numerator in the first term is positive. Tobin has shown that if the distribution of y is completely specified by y^* and σ_y^2 and if we further assume that $y - y^*/\sigma_y$ has the same distribution with mean zero and variance unity, then this is sufficient to establish that

$$\frac{\partial^2 \sigma_y^2}{\partial (y^*)^2} \leq 0 \tag{4.15}$$

so that in general these indifference curves are concave in the y^* direction in the (y^*, σ_y^2) plane.[1]

To complete the specification of the participant's decision problem we need to determine the set of points (y^*, σ_y^2) available for different choices of the control variable F. From (4.1) we have that

$$y = F(r - R) + Wi. \tag{4.16}$$

We assume that the participant has an expected value of R, which we designate R^*, and a variance of R, which we designate σ_R^2, both of which are conditional on past values of R. The difference between the forward rate r and the expected value of R, R^*, is called the term premium, T; that is

$$T \equiv r - R^*. \tag{4.17}$$

From (4.16) and (4.17) we see that the expected value of y, y^*, is

$$y^* = FT + Wi^*, \tag{4.18}$$

where i^* is the expected value of i. Hence, T provides an incentive for taking long forward positions if positive and short positions if negative.

If the participant has a joint distribution for R and P with means R^* and P^*, variances σ_R^2 and σ_P^2, and covariance σ_{RP}, then rewriting y as

$$y = Fr + (W - F)R - WP \tag{4.19}$$

it is clear, since F and r are fixed, that the variance of y is given by

$$\sigma_y^2 = (W - F)^2 \sigma_R^2 - 2W(W - F)\sigma_{RP} + W^2 \sigma_P^2, \tag{4.20}$$

which is quadratic in each of F and W. Note that if the participant enters into no forward contracts, we have

$$\begin{aligned} \sigma_y^2 &= W^2(\sigma_R^2 - 2\sigma_{RP} + \sigma_P^2) \\ &= W^2(\sigma_i^2), \end{aligned} \tag{4.21}$$

where σ_i^2 is the variance of i. The term *hedging* refers to entering into forward contracts that anticipate future commitments. In the present context this means taking a long forward position if the participant anticipates future spot investment (i.e., $W > 0$) and a short position if future spot borrowing is anticipated (i.e., $W < 0$). A *fully hedged* portfolio is one for which F is set equal to W. Using (4.20), the variance of real income for the fully hedged portfolio is

$$\sigma_y^2 = W^2 \sigma_P^2. \tag{4.22}$$

By hedging his portfolio fully, the participant has protected himself from uncertainty of nominal interest rates and is exposed only to the uncertainty of price-level changes. We shall assume in this analysis that hedges against price-level changes are not available to the participant.

Note that the fully hedged portfolio offers less variance of real income only if $\sigma_P^2 < \sigma_i^2$, requiring that the variance of price changes be less than variance in the real interest rate. Minimizing σ_y^2 with respect to F by setting the derivative $d\sigma_y^2/dF$ equal to zero, we find that the variance-minimizing value of F, denoted $\tilde{F}$, is given by

$$\tilde{F} = W\left(\frac{\sigma_R^2 - \sigma_{RP}}{\sigma_R^2}\right). \tag{4.23}$$

This indicates that for positive σ_{RP}, $\tilde{F}$ is less than W, meaning that a minimum-risk forward position is one of partial hedging rather than full hedging. In effect $\tilde{F}$ offers diversification between risk in the real interest rate and risk in price-level change associated with unhedged and fully hedged portfolios, respectively. If σ_{RP} were large enough so that $\sigma_{RP} > \sigma_R^2$, then $\tilde{F} < 0$, and the participant would take a forward position opposite in sign to W for minimum risk. It would seem that the case $\sigma_{RP} > 0$ is most likely to correspond with reality.

RESPONSE TO CHANGES IN THE
TERM PREMIUM: INCOME AND
SUBSTITUTION EFFECTS

Recalling from (4.18) that expected real income is given by

$$y^* = FT + Wi^*, \tag{4.24}$$

we note that the participant has an incentive to increase F if T is positive and to decrease F if T is negative. Since expected utility is an increasing function of y^* and a decreasing function of σ_y^2, we might expect that for $T \neq 0$ the participant would choose $F > \tilde{F}$ for $T > 0$ and $F < \tilde{F}$ for $T < 0$, accepting a level of risk above the minimum in return for increased expected real income.

The locus of combinations of expected real income and risk available to the participant may be obtained by substituting the expression for F from (4.24), namely

$$F = \frac{y^* - Wi^*}{T}, \tag{4.25}$$

into the expression for σ_y^2 (4.20). This yields

$$\sigma_y^2 = \sigma_R^2 \left(\frac{y^*}{T}\right)^2 - 2W[\sigma_R^2 Z - \sigma_{RP}]\left(\frac{y^*}{T}\right) + W^2[\sigma_R^2 Z^2 - 2\sigma_{RP}Z + \sigma_P^2], \tag{4.26}$$

where

$$Z = 1 + \frac{i^*}{T}. \tag{4.27}$$

Thus σ_y^2 is quadratic in each of y^*, $1/T$, i^* (since it is quadratic in Z), and W. This function is illustrated for fixed values of $T > 0$ (say T_1), i^*, and $W > 0$ by the parabola C_1 in Figure 4-1. The function σ_y^2 has a minimum at the value of y given by

$$\tilde{y}_1^* = \tilde{F}T_1 + Wi^*, \qquad (4.28)$$

where $\tilde{F}$ is the variance-minimizing forward position given by (4.23), for which we assume $\sigma_R^2 > \sigma_{RP} > 0$, so that $W > \tilde{F} > 0$. Note that y_1^* is positive since we have taken W and T_1 to be positive.

The positively sloped curves in Figure 4-1 represent indifference curves derived from $U^*(y^*, \sigma_y^2)$. Expected utility is maximized at a point such as A_1 on C_1, where the indifference curve of highest attainable utility is tangent to the quadratic constraint. Note that a level of risk above the minimum has

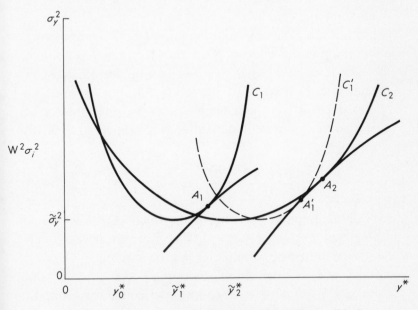

FIGURE 4 – 1   Income and Substitution Effects, $T > 0$

been accepted in return for some increase in expected real income. This may represent a choice for F either greater or less than a fully hedged position, W.

Consider the effect of an increase in T_1 to T_2. Since the quadratic constraint is a function of $1/T$ a change in T will alter the shape of the constraint. We shall show that the new constraint is of the form C_2 in Figure 4-1. In Figure 4-1 the point $(y_0^*, W^2\sigma_i^2)$ indicates expected real income and associated variance at $F = 0$ (an unhedged portfolio). y_0^* is positive since W is positive. The minimum-risk level of y^* on C_1 occurs at $\tilde{y}_1^* > y_0^*$ since we assume $\tilde{F} > 0$. Substituting the expression for $\tilde{F}$, (4.23), into that for σ_y^2, (4.20), we have that the minimum variance attainable is

$$\tilde{\sigma}_y^2 = W^2(\sigma_{RP}^2\sigma_R^2 - 2\sigma_{RP}^2 + \sigma_P^2), \qquad (4.29)$$

which is independent of T. The variance for y_0^*, namely $W^2\sigma_i^2$, is also independent of T. Hence if T is changed, the new constraint must pass through the point $(y_0^*, W^2\sigma_i^2)$ and reach a minimum at the value $\tilde{\sigma}_y^2$. Since the change in T is positive, the new level of y^* giving minimum risk, say $\tilde{y}_2^*$, must be greater than $\tilde{y}_1^*$ because of relation (4.28).

The slope of C_2 is greater (less negative) than that of C_1 at the point y_0^* since the derivative with respect to T of the slope $\partial\sigma_y^2/\partial y^*$ is

$$\frac{\partial(\partial\sigma_y^2/\partial y^*)}{\partial T} = \frac{2W}{T^2}(\sigma_R^2 - \sigma_{RP}) > 0 \qquad (4.30)$$

by our assumption $\sigma_R^2 - \sigma_{RP} > 0$, which is equivalent to saying that $\tilde{F} > 0$, or $\tilde{y}_2^* > \tilde{y}_1^*$. The same proposition may be demonstrated by a simple geometric argument. The constraints are of the form $C_1 = a_1 y^{*2} + b_1 y^* + c_1$ and $C_2 = a_2 y^{*2} + b_2 y^* + c_2$. Points of intersection are given the two solutions to the quadratic equation $C_2 - C_1 = (a_2 - a_1)y^{*2} + (b_2 - b_1)y^* + (c_2 - c_1) = 0$. One of these points of intersection is between the minimizing points $\tilde{y}_1^*$ and $\tilde{y}_2^*$. The other must be in the negative direction from $\tilde{y}_1^*$ since given that $a_2 - a_1 < 0$ there is always some $y^* < \tilde{y}_1^*$ for which $C_1 - C_2 < 0$. Hence, going in the negative direction from $\tilde{y}_1^*$, C_1 must cut C_2 from below at a value of y^* (in this case y_0^*) that is less than $\tilde{y}_1^*$. Thus the new constraint will be of the form of parabola C_2 in Figure 4–1.

Associated with constraint C_2 in Figure 4–1 is a new expected utility-maximizing choice of y^* and σ_y^2 at point A_2, where the constraint is tangent to the highest attainable indifference curve. We may distinguish two separate components in the move from A_1 to A_2. These will be called *income* and *substitution* effects, which require special definitions in this context.

Arrow has suggested that willingness to engage in wagers of some given variance and expected return should increase with income.[2] If the opposite were the case, then wealthy individuals would hold very small absolute amounts of risky assets. This tendency to increase holdings of risky assets as income rises is called declining absolute risk aversion. In our context this amounts to saying that indifference curves become more positively sloped as one moves in the direction of higher expected real income, y^*, at a fixed level of variance, σ_y^2. Hence, if we were to displace the constraint, C_1, horizontally through the indifference field, say to C_1', in Figure 4–1 (tangent to the indifference curve containing A_2), we would have a new equilibrium combination at A_1' corresponding to a higher level of income variance (and, hence, F) than at A_1. This amounts to offering the same rate for combining variance and income (for given variance) but at higher expected income. This hypothetical shift from A_1 to A_1' is what we shall call the income effect and it arises from the assumption of declining absolute risk aversion.

The remaining shift from A_1' to A_2 along the indifference curve in Figure 4–1 we shall call the substitution effect, and it is in the direction of greater σ_y^2 and y^* and hence larger F. This is a result of the new constraint, C_2, making increases in y^* cheaper in terms of σ_y^2 since its slope is less than that of C_1' for given σ_y^2. This is assured by the second derivative of C_1 being greater than that of C_2, i.e., $2\sigma_R^2/T_1^2 > 2\sigma_R^2/T_2^2$ since $T_2 > T_1$. Thus an increase in T results in a substitution effect in the direction of larger F.

If the initial value of T, T_1, is negative, the participant holding a positive portfolio ($W > 0$) pays a cost in terms of expected income to achieve minimum risk at forward position $\tilde{F} > 0$. This situation is illustrated in Figure 4–2 by constraint C_1 associated with T_1, which passes through the point $(y_0^*, W^2\sigma_i^2)$ corresponding to the forward position $F = 0$ and which has a minimum at expected income $\tilde{y}_1^* < y_0^*$ (since $\tilde{F} > 0$ and $T_1 < 0$) and minimum variance $\tilde{\sigma}_y^2$. Expected utility is maximized at the tangency point A_1. Note that at A_1 expected income is less than the unhedged income y_0^*, indicating that the participant has taken a long forward posi-

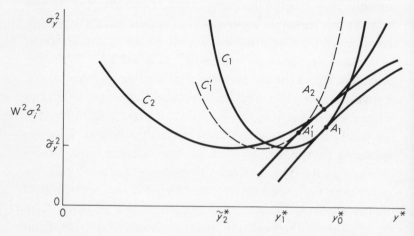

FIGURE 4 – 2   Income and Substitution Effects, $T < 0$

tion, which offers some reduction in risk (from that for $F = 0$) but at the cost of reduced expected income. A less risk-averse individual, that is, one with more steeply sloped indifference curves (requiring less increase in y^* for given increase in σ_y^2), might have chosen a point on C_1 offering greater income and variance than point $(y_0^*, W^2\sigma_i^2)$, thus corresponding to a short forward position.

If T takes on a new value, T_2, that is less than T_1, then a new constraint such as C_2 faces the portfolio holder. The shift from A_1 to the new equilibrium point A_2 may again be decomposed into income and substitution effects. The income effect is given in Figure 4-2 by displacing the original constraint, C_1, through the indifference field until it is tangent at A_1' at position C_1' to the indifference curve containing A_2. This amounts to offering, hypothetically, the same rates of combination of y^* and σ_y^2 (at given σ_y^2) but at lower levels of y^*. Following our assumption that the slope of indifference curves (at given σ_y^2) varies directly with expected income, A_1' indicates a reduction in σ_y^2 and hence an increase in F (to bring it closer to $\tilde{F}$, the risk-minimizing value). The remaining part of the shift, from A_1' to A_2, is the substitution effect. This is in the direction of greater expected income and variance, since C_2 allows the participant to gain expected income at less cost in variance (for fixed σ_y^2) as compared to C_1'. The substitution effect, then, implies a reduction in F. In the case illustrated by Figure 4-2 the substitution is larger than the income effect, so that a change in T in the negative direction has induced the portfolio-holder to reduce his forward position, F. Viewing a negative T as a cost of hedging, this amounts to saying that an increase in that cost reduces the amount of hedging protection purchased.

If the participant in the preceding example had taken a short forward position prior to the constraint shifting to C_2, then both income and substitution effects favor increasing his short position. This is evident from the fact that at all y^* greater than y_0^* (i.e., for short positions), C_2 offers greater expected income at any given level of variance. In summary, then, when term premiums, T, are negative, the number of forward-loan contracts supplied by holders of positive portfolios is reduced as the term premium becomes more negative.

RESPONSE TO CHANGES IN THE LEVEL OF INTEREST RATES

In our analysis of the choice of an optimal forward position, we have taken the third and higher central moments of y to be zero, so that only mean and variance, as functions of F, have been relevant to the maximization of expected utility. However, if participants have the alternative of holding cash at negligible cost, then bonds will be purchased only at nonnegative nominal interest rates. This is because cash is a substitute for bonds offering a zero nominal rate of return (and offers greater liquidity). Hence there is effectively a reflecting barrier at zero in the movement of R. Potential declines in R become increasingly small at low levels of R_{-1}, while sharp increases remain possible. Thus the conditional distribution of R becomes skewed in the positive direction at low levels of R_{-1}.

Since y is a linear function of R_{-1}, the distribution of y must also be skewed. The distribution of y may now be specified by mean, y^*, variance, σ_y^2, and the third central moment, σ_y^3 (as a measure of skewness). Expression (4.6) for expected utility becomes

$$U^* = U(y^*) + \tfrac{1}{2}U''(y^*)\sigma_y^2 + \tfrac{1}{6}U'''(y^*)\sigma_y^3. \qquad (4.31)$$

U^* may now be written as

$$U^* = U^*(y^*, \sigma_y^2, \sigma_y^3), \qquad (4.32)$$

and we note that from (4.6) and our assumption (4.4) we have

$$\frac{\partial U^*}{\partial \sigma_y^3} = \frac{1}{6}U'''(y^*) > 0. \qquad (4.33)$$

The decision problem facing the participant is the maximization of U^* over choices of F that determine the locus of attainable points $(y^*, \sigma_y^2, \sigma_y^3)$, a surface in three-dimensional space.

To reduce this problem to one that is amenable to two-dimensional graphical analysis, we construct an index of subjective risk in the following way. Consider a mapping, S_y, of pairs (σ_y^2, σ_y^3) into the real numbers such that

$$S_y(\sigma_y^2, \sigma_y^3) = S_y(\sigma_y^{2'}, \sigma_y^{3'}) \qquad (4.34)$$

if and only if

$$U^*(y^*, \sigma_y^2, \sigma_y^3) = U^*(y^*, \sigma_y^{2'}, \sigma_y^{3'}), \qquad (4.35)$$

denoted $U^*(y^*, S_y)$. The real numbers S_y are ordered so that $S_y > S_y'$ means that $U^*(y^*, S_y) < U^*(y^*, S_y')$. Each $U^*(y^*, S_y)$ represents an indifference locus in the (σ_y^2, σ_y^3) plane, the slope of which is given by

$$\frac{\partial \sigma_y^2}{\partial \sigma_y^3} = -\frac{3U''(y^*)}{U'''(y^*)}, \qquad (4.36)$$

which is positive by conditions (4.2), (4.3), and (4.4). Thus, holding y^* constant, a given S_y represents pairs (σ_y^2, σ_y^3), which lie on a straight line that has the slope given by (4.36). If we take this slope to be fixed over different y^*, then we may apply the function S_y without regard to income level. Indifference curves may be defined in the (y^*, S_y) plane and these have the slope

$$\frac{\partial S_y}{\partial y^*} = \frac{-\partial U^*/\partial y^*}{\partial U^*/\partial S_y} > 0 \qquad (4.37)$$

by (4.11) and the ordering of S_y.

It will be convenient to interpret S_y as subjective risk, a composite measure of variance and skewness that is filtered, so to speak, through the participant's utility function. The level of S_y will depend on the forward position taken. Income is composed, as we saw in (4.1), of gains on forward contracts, $F(r - R)$, plus the amount that would be earned on an unhedged portfolio, $W(R - P)$. Remember that we have assumed only that the distribution of R is skewed in the positive direction. At $F = 0$, $\sigma_R^3 > 0$ and $y = W(R - P)$, which means that income is skewed in a positive direction, $\sigma_y^3 > 0$. However, at $F = W$, $y = W(r - P)$, so $\sigma_y^3 = 0$. At $F > W$, $\sigma_R^3 > 0$, and $y = W(r - P) + (F - W)(r - R)$, which means that substantial losses may occur in the second term in y on a long forward position while gains are limited by the floor on R; hence $\sigma_y^3 < 0$. Combining this framework with the knowledge from (4.20) that σ_y^2 is quadratic in F, we may take curve C_1 in Figure 4–3 as a heuristic example of the relationship between S_y and F. The above considerations would suggest that C_1 reaches a minimum at some $F < W$ and rises monotonically from there.

Suppose that the general level of interest rates rises from the level applicable for C_1. This means that σ_R^3 is reduced since the zero floor is farther from the current level. The relationship between S_y and F will shift to a position such as that of C_2. Comparing C_2 to C_1, at $F = 0$, $y = W(R - P)$, so that the distribution of y becomes less highly skewed in

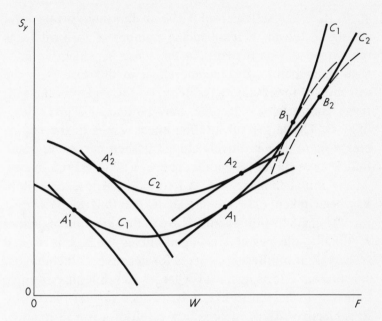

FIGURE 4-3 Response of Future Lenders to Rise in Level of Interest Rates

the positive direction. At $F = W$, $y = W(r - P)$, so that, as for C_1, the only uncertainty is in P, and S_y is unchanged. At $F > W$, $y = W(r - P) + (F - W)(r - R)$, and while substantial losses may occur in the second term in y, potential gains have become less restricted in comparison to those at the higher interest-rate level and the distribution of y less skewed in the negative direction. These considerations suggest that C_2 is above C_1 at $F < W$—it intersects C_1 at $F = W$—and below C_1 at $F > W$.

Indifference curves in the (y^*, S_y) plane may be translated into the (F, S_y) plane by replacing y^* by the F corresponding to it for given L, C^*, and W. The solid and positively sloped curves in Figure 4-3 tangent to C_1 and C_2 represent indifference curves for L positive. The shift in tangencies from

A_1 to A_2 has resulted from a rise in the interest-rate level and indicates an increase in the number of forward loans offered by the participant. In the sense in which we have used them before, the income effect in this case is in the direction of fewer contracts offered (in the region of the shift fewer contracts, less income, may be had at a given level of risk). The larger substitution effect results in the net increase in F. The positively sloped dashed curves represent indifference curves for another hedger who is less risk-averse. At the initial tangency, B_1, a long position in excess of W has been taken that is enlarged in the shift to B_2 on C_2. Income and substitution effects are in the direction of greater F. Finally, the negatively sloped curves tangent at A_1' and A_2' represent indifference curves for negative T. Income and substitution effects again favor larger F. While this example is meant to be illustrative only, it does suggest that a rise in subjective risk of income as a result of a rise in nominal interest rates may increase the number of forward loans offered by participants. This agrees with the intuitively appealing proposition that as interest-rate risk rises, portfolios should become more fully hedged.

SPECULATORS AND FUTURE BORROWERS

The decision problem facing participants for whom $W = 0$ (*speculators*) and $W < 0$ (future borrowers) may easily be seen to be special cases of the problem for future lenders. Variance of expected gain from holding forward contracts for the speculator is simply $F^2\sigma_R^2$, where F is the net long position of a speculator, so that income variance is incurred symmetrically on either side of the market. Our analysis for the future lender, then, follows through for the speculator.

Future borrowers are participants for whom W is negative. The structure of the decision problem for the future borrower is the same as that for the future lender since only the sign of W has changed. Hedging for these participants consists of taking a short position so that forward funds are available for future needs. Real income or, if negative, cost is given by expression (4.1), its expected value by (4.18), its variance by (4.20), and the constraint on choices of y^* and σ_y^2 by (4.25). The minimum-risk forward position is given by $\tilde{F}$ in (4.23) but now represents the fraction $(\sigma_R^2 - \sigma_{RP})/\sigma_R^2$ of a negative W, that is, a forward position.

Figure 4-1 may be used to investigate the response of a future borrower's forward position to a change in the term premium, T, from a negative value, T_1, to a more negative value T_2. Mentally shifting the y^* axis so that the unhedged income, y_0^*, occurs at a negative value of y^*, we note that for negative T_1, forward position $\tilde{F}$ corresponds to a minimum variance y^* on C_1, namely $\tilde{y}_1^*$, that is greater than y_0^*. A fall in T to T_2 shifts the constraint to C_2. As in the example for $W > 0$, the participant shifts his choice of y^* and σ_y^2 from A_1 to A_2 with income and substitution effects being in the direction of greater y^* and σ_y^2 and hence more negative F. In similar fashion, Figure 4-2 serves to illustrate a shift in T from a positive value, T_1, associated with constraint C_1, to a larger value, T_2, and constraint C_2. In this case, minimum risk y^* occurs at $\tilde{y}_1^*$ on C_1, which is less than unhedged y^*, y_0^*. Thus, T_1 represents a cost in assuming minimum-variance forward position $\tilde{F}$. An increase in T to T_2 causes the constraint to shift to C_2 and the participant's forward position to shift from A_1 on C_1 to A_2 on C_2. A_2 represents a larger σ_y^2 and hence a smaller forward position. This results from an income effect in the direction of a larger forward position and a substitution effect, larger than the income effect, that is in the direction of a smaller forward position. Thus, for the future borrower, as for the future lender, the forward position taken varies directly with T.

The response of the future borrower to interest-rate level is illustrated in Figure 4–4. Constraint C_1 represents the available choices between subjective risk and net long forward position at a low interest-rate level, C_2, at a higher level. The positively sloped curves tangent at A_1 and A_2 reflect both income and substitution effects in the direction of positive F. The shift from A_1' to A_2', tangencies on the negatively sloped solid indifference curves for negative T, reflects an income effect toward more negative F and a stronger substitution effect toward less negative F. Finally, the dashed negatively sloped indifference curves for a less risk-averse individual produce a shift to less negative F, B_1 to B_2. Income and substitution effects are in the direction of less negative F.

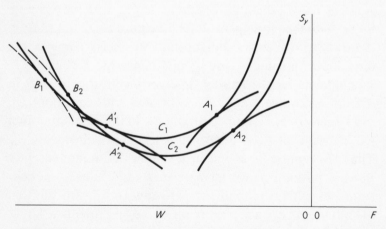

FIGURE 4 – 4   Response of Future Borrowers to Rise in Level of Interest Rates

NET SUPPLY OF FORWARD LOANS

Thus far we have assumed that a participant may cover a forward position that exceeds the amount of his portfolio by borrowing at the going (default-free) spot rate. In reality, many participants on the long side of the forward market (including financial institutions such as banks, which in this framework are loan-brokers who also speculate in the forward market) will experience varying credit availability and thus cost in covering forward positions according to the level of business confidence. Thus we might expect that the supply of forward loans would be positively related to an indicator of business confidence.

In our discussion of the forward market we have considered the response in the net supply of forward loans to changes in term premiums, the level of interest rates, and business confidence. Individual net supply may then be expressed by the function

$$F = F(T,I,Z), \tag{4.38}$$

where I is the current level of interest rates and Z is an indicator of the level of business confidence. The analysis has suggested that the signs of the partial derivatives of F are as follows:

$$\frac{\partial F}{\partial T} > 0,$$

$$\frac{\partial F}{\partial I} > 0, \tag{4.39}$$

and

$$\frac{\partial F}{\partial Z} > 0.$$

These implications of the analysis provide the basis for constructing a testable model of the cyclical movement of the term structure.

AGGREGATION OF INDIVIDUAL SUPPLY FUNCTIONS

Let us assume that the excess supply function (4.38) is linear in the variables T, I, and Z. Using the subscript i to denote coefficients and variables pertaining to the ith individual, the excess supply of forward loans for that individual may be written as

$$F_i = a_i + b_i I + c_i Z + d_i T_i. \tag{4.40}$$

The subscript i on the term premium provides for the possibility that individuals may differ in their expectations of future spot rates and hence have individually perceived term premiums. The signs of the partial derivatives of the excess supply functions given by (4.39) imply that the signs of b_i, c_i, and d_i are positive.

Presumably the variables T, I, and Z do not capture all the factors affecting individual excess supply. We shall assume that such left-out variables enter the supply relationship as an additive stochastic disturbance, f_i, which is a function of these variables. Under this assumption we have

$$F_i = a_i + b_i I + c_i Z + d_i T_i + f_i. \tag{4.41}$$

Since the effect of given left-out variables may persist from period to period, we might expect there to be serial correlation in the disturbances.

Denoting the expectation held by the ith individual as R_i^*, we have defined T_i as

$$T_i = r - R_i^*. \tag{4.42}$$

Suppose that there is an average of expectations, R^*, in the sense that

$$R_i^* = m_i + n_i R^*, \tag{4.43}$$

where, if N is the total number of market participants, we have

$$\sum_{i=1}^{N} m_i = 0, \tag{4.44}$$

and

$$\frac{\sum_{i=1}^{N} n_i}{N} = 1. \tag{4.45}$$

Hence, R^*, as we have defined it, is just the arithmetic average of all individual expectations.

Let us next aggregate individual excess supplies, F_i, over the N individuals to obtain a market-clearing equation for r. We have then that

$$\sum_{i=1}^{N} F_i = 0 \tag{4.46}$$

$$= \sum_{i=1}^{N} a_i + I \sum_{i=1}^{N} b_i + Z \sum_{i=1}^{N} c_i + \sum_{i=1}^{N} d_i(r - R_i^*) + \sum_{i=1}^{N} f_i.$$

Denoting the sum of any coefficient over N individuals by the subscript N, for example, $\Sigma_{i=1}^{N} a_i = a_N$, we may rewrite (4.46) as

$$-\sum_{i=1}^{N} d_i(r - R_i^*) = a_N + b_N I + c_N Z + f_N, \tag{4.47}$$

or equivalently

$$-r\sum_{i=1}^{N} d_i = a_N + b_N I + c_N Z - \sum_{i=1}^{N} d_i R_i^* + f_N. \qquad (4.48)$$

Dividing each side by $-\Sigma_{i=1}^{N} d_i$, denoted $-d_N$, we obtain

$$r = -\frac{a_N}{d_N} - \frac{b_N}{d_N}I - \frac{c_N}{d_N}Z + \frac{\displaystyle\sum_{i=1}^{N} d_i R_i^*}{d_N} - \frac{f_N}{d_N}. \qquad (4.49)$$

Substituting $m_i + n_i R^*$ for R_i^* from (4.43) gives us

$$r = -\frac{a_N}{d_N} - \frac{b_N}{d_N}I - \frac{c_N}{d_N}Z + \frac{\displaystyle\sum_{i=1}^{N} d_i m_i}{d_N} + R^* \frac{\displaystyle\sum_{i=1}^{N} d_i n_i}{d_N} - \frac{f_N}{d_N} \qquad (4.50)$$

Note that d_i is the response in forward loans offered by individual i to a change in the perceived term premium. Our analysis relates this response to the individual's expected utility of income. The coefficients m_i and n_i relate the individual's expectation to the average of individual expectations. It would seem reasonable to assume that there is no relationship, on average, between characteristics of an individual's utility function, including the coefficient d_i, and the position of his expectation relative to the average, as determined by m_i and n_i. By this we mean that the covariances of d_i and m_i and of d_i and n_i across the sample of all market participants are zero. This implies along with assumptions (4.44) and (4.45) that

$$\frac{\displaystyle\sum_{i=1}^{N} d_i(m_i - 0)}{N} = \frac{\displaystyle\sum_{i=1}^{N} d_i m_i}{N} = 0, \qquad (4.51)$$

hence

$$\sum_{i=1}^{N} d_i m_i = 0, \tag{4.52}$$

and that

$$\frac{\sum_{i=1}^{N} d_i(n_i - 1)}{N} = \frac{\sum_{i=1}^{N} d_i n_i - d_N}{N} = 0, \tag{4.53}$$

hence

$$\sum_{i=1}^{N} d_i n_i = d_N. \tag{4.54}$$

Using conditions (4.52) and (4.54) to simplify (4.50) we obtain

$$r = -\frac{a_N}{d_N} - \frac{b_N}{d_N} I - \frac{c_N}{d_N} Z + 1R^* - \frac{f_N}{d_N}. \tag{4.55}$$

Simplifying notation, (4.50) may be rewritten in the form

$$r = a + bI + cZ + R^* + f. \tag{4.56}$$

The positive signs of the individual b_i, c_i, and d_i imply that coefficients b and c are negative.

The quantity $r - R^*$ may be thought of as the equilibrium average, or equilibrium market, term premium and, re-arranging (4.56), is given by

$$T = a + bI + cZ + f. \tag{4.57}$$

The analysis presented thus far has been done in the framework of a single future time period. Under the assumptions that expected utility of income in future time periods is the sum of expected utility for each future period and that the participant ignores intermediate gains or losses on forward contracts prior to their being exercised, our model may be generalized to determine the equilibrium term premium for each future period. In this case, the term premium established in the forward market at time t for loans n periods ahead, denoted by $_tT_{t+n}$, is given by

$$_tT_{t+n} = a_n + b_nI_t + c_nZ_t + f_{n,t},\qquad (4.58)$$

where term subscripts, n, have been added to the constants and time subscripts, t, to the variables. If the above assumptions are not met and there is interaction between forward-position decisions for different future periods, then presumably the demand for forward contracts for future period $t + n$ would depend on the entire set of term premiums, $\{_tT_{t+i}\}$. Expression (4.58) for equilibrium $_tT_{t+n}$ might then be viewed as a reduced-form equation giving $_tT_{t+n}$ in terms of variables exogenous to the forward market in loans.

MEASUREMENT OF MARKET EXPECTATIONS

Clearly no direct data exist from which the average of individual expectations may be computed. Consequently, we propose to decompose the market expectation into a component that is the expectation conditional on the history of the spot-rate sequence and another component that is a random disturbance with mean zero representing the effect on the market expectation of information independent of the history of spot rates. The first component will be simulated empirically as the conditional expectation implied by a discrete linear stochastic process fitted to the relevant sequence of one-period spot rates. Denoting the first component by $_t\widehat{R}^*_{t+n}$ and the second by $w_{n,t}$, the market expectation is given by

$$_tR^*_{t+n} = {_t\widehat{R}^*_{t+n}} + w_{n,t}.\qquad (4.59)$$

Substituting (4.59) into (4.58) we obtain

$$_tr_{t+n} - {_t\widehat{R}^*_{t+n}} = a_n + b_nI_t + c_nZ_t + (w_{n,t} + f_{n,t}) \quad (4.60)$$

in which the dependent variable is an estimate of the equilibrium term premium. The identification and fitting of discrete linear processes appropriate to the sequence of one-year yields in the Durand data and the computation of implied conditional expectations are described in Chapter 5.

Notes

1. James Tobin, "Liquidity Preference as Behavior Towards Risk," *The Review of Economic Studies* 25 (February 1958): 65–86. See also M. S. Feldstein, "Mean-Variance Analysis in the Theory of Liquidity Preference and Portfolio Selection," *The Review of Economic Studies* 36 (January 1969): 5–12.
2. Arrow, *Theory of Risk Bearing,* pp. 33–35.

Representation of the Durand Annual One-year Rates as a Discrete Linear Stochastic Process

INTRODUCTION

Representation of the one-year spot rates from the Durand data as a discrete linear stochastic process will play a central role in our tests of the model of the term structure developed in Chapter 4. Conditional expectations of future one-year spot rates are used in Chapter 6 in conjunction with forward rates of the corresponding horizon to construct estimates of term premiums as suggested in Chapter 4. The linear process representation is also important in the interpretation of results presented in Chapter 7, where the term-premium model is tested in an error-learning framework.

This chapter outlines the general procedure for empirical representation of a time series as a linear stochastic process, presents the particular results obtained in the case of the Durand one-year spot rates, and describes the computation of the implied conditional expectations of future one-year spot rates.[1]

IDENTIFICATION OF LINEAR
PROCESS MODELS AND ESTIMATION
OF PARAMETERS

In Chapter 2 we described a class of discrete linear stochastic processes of the form

$$\phi_p(B)(1 - B)^d R_t = \theta_0 + \theta_q(B)u_t, \qquad (5.1)$$

which we called an integrated autoregressive–moving-average process of order (p,d,q), where $\phi_p(B)$ is a polynomial of degree p in the backshift operator B, $\theta_q(B)$ is a polynomial of degree q in B, θ_0 is a constant, and the u_t are independent, identically distributed random variables of zero mean and variance σ_u^2. The identification of such a process as a model to describe the behavior of an empirical time series is the determination of the dimensions (p,d,q). This is accomplished with the aid of the sample autocorrelations of the R_t and their differences. Since we require that both $\phi_p(B)$ and $\theta_q(B)$ have roots outside the unit circle, the process (5.1) may be thought of as a stationary process in the series $(1 - B)^d R_t$. The autocorrelations of a nonstationary series do not die off with increasing lag. Hence the series under investigation is differenced, say d times, until the autocorrelations do die off. The dth difference of the series may then be thought of as a stationary series of the class described by (5.1). It remains then to use the sample autocorrelations of the series $(1 - B)^d R_t$ to identify the dimensions p and q.

Autocorrelations from purely autoregressive processes "tail off," while those of a moving average process cut off abruptly. A mixed process produces autocorrelations with these characteristics combined: an irregular pattern through lag q, then tailing off. The theoretical autocorrelations, ρ_k, of a pure autoregressive process follow the recursive relationship

$$\phi_p(B)\rho_k = 0 \tag{5.2}$$

so that

$$\rho_k = \phi_1\rho_{k-1} + \cdots + \phi_p\rho_{k-p}, \tag{5.3}$$

where the ϕ_i, $i = 1, \ldots, p$, are the coefficients in the polynomial $\phi_p(B)$. For a first-order autoregressive process

$$\rho_k = \phi_1^k. \tag{5.4}$$

Hence the autocorrelations of a first-order autoregressive process decline exponentially. The general solution for ρ_k is

$$\rho_k = A_1 G_1^k + A_2 G_2^k + \cdots + A_p G_p^k, \tag{5.5}$$

where the G_i^{-1} are the roots of the characteristic equation $\phi_p(B) = 0$ and the A_i are given by initial conditions. Expression (5.5) is called the autocorrelation function of the process. When a pair of the roots G_i^{-1} is complex, the autocorrelation function will contain a damped sine wave, and the series will exhibit pseudoperiodic behavior.

The autocovariance of lag k for a pure moving-average process is given by

$$
\begin{aligned}
E[(Z_t - EZ_t)&(Z_{t-k} - EZ_{t-k})] \\
&= E[(u_t - \theta_1 u_{t-1} - \cdots - \theta_q u_{t-q}) \\
&\quad (u_{t-k} - \theta_1 u_{t-k-1} - \cdots - \theta_q u_{t-k-q})],
\end{aligned} \tag{5,6}
$$

from which the autocorrelations are given by

$$
\rho_k = \begin{cases}
\dfrac{-\theta_k + \theta_1\theta_{k-1} + \cdots + \theta_{q-k}\theta_q}{1 + \theta_1^2 + \cdots + \theta_q^2}, & k = 1, \ldots, q, \\
0, & k > q.
\end{cases} \tag{5.7}
$$

Graphically, the autocorrelation function will consist of a sequence of spikes at lags $k = 1, \ldots, q$, and zeros for $k > q$.

Expressions for the autocovariance functions of mixed autoregressive–moving-average processes are more complex.

For $p = 1$, $q = 1$, for example,

$$\rho_1 = \frac{(1 - \phi_1\theta_1)(\phi_1 - \theta_1)}{(1 + \theta_1^2 - 2\phi_1\theta_1)} \tag{5.8}$$

and

$$\rho_k = \rho_1\theta^{k-1}, \qquad k > 1. \tag{5.9}$$

In general, the moving-average terms will enter into the first q autocorrelations. For lags greater than q, the autocorrelations will follow the recursive relationship $\phi_p(B)\rho_k = 0$ $(k > q)$, as they would if the process were purely auto-regressive with polynomial $\phi_p(B)$.

From the known properties of the theoretical autocorrelation functions for various types of processes, we may hope to identify the dimensions p and q for a given body of data by examining its sample autocorrelations. Estimated standard errors for the autocorrelations are available from Bartlett's formula with the estimated ρ_v, r_v, inserted for theoretical values.[2] Bartlett's formula is

$$\mathrm{Var}(r_j) \approx \frac{1}{n} \sum_{v=-\infty}^{+\infty} \rho_v^2, \tag{5.10}$$

so that under the hypothesis that the autocorrelations after some lag k are zero,

$$\mathrm{Var}(r_j) \approx \frac{1}{n}[1 + 2(r_1^2 + \cdots + r_k^2)], \qquad j > k. \tag{5.11}$$

The square root of this expression provides an estimate of the standard deviation of r_j.

Preliminary estimates for the parameters may be derived from the theoretical relationships between the ρ_i and the parameters for a given tentative choice of (p,d,q). These preliminary estimates are useful in the exploratory stage of looking at various data series and provide starting values in the parameter space for use in iterative procedures in estimation.

In the second step of fitting the general model, parameters are estimated for a given identification. If the disturbances, u_t, are normal and independently distributed, maximum-likelihood estimates of the parameters are obtained by minimizing the sum of squared residuals, $\Sigma \widehat{u}_t^2$, over the parameters $\phi_1, \ldots, \phi_p, \theta_0, \theta_1, \ldots, \theta_q$. Approximate standard errors for the parameter estimates are computed from a quadratic approximation to the sum-of-squares surface in the region of the maximum-likelihood estimates.

In discussion of the identification and estimation results, we shall adopt a compact notation for designation of the models. The general integrated autoregressive–moving-average model of dimensions (p,d,q) will be denoted by ARIMA(p,d,q). For subcases, the appropriate initials and dimension places are dropped. For example, an ARIMA$(0,d,q)$ model is just IMA(d,q), which is of the form

$$(1 - B)^d Z_t = \theta_q(B)u_t. \tag{5.12}$$

APPLICATION OF THE IDENTIFICATION PROCEDURE TO THE DURAND ONE-YEAR SPOT RATES

The sample autocorrelations for various differences of the one-year spot-rate series were computed as follows: for the kth lag

$$r_k = \frac{C_0}{C_k}, \tag{5.13}$$

where

$$C_k = \frac{1}{n} \sum_{t=1}^{n-k} (X_t - \bar{X})(X_{t+k} - \bar{X}), \qquad (5.14)$$

and X_t denotes some order of difference of the original series. The results of these computations are presented in Figures 5-1 and 5-2 for the original series, given in Table 5-1, and its first difference. The distribution of sample autocorrelations whose theoretical value is zero is sufficiently close to the normal so that comparison of some r_j with its standard deviation computed from formula (5.11) using the values of r_1 through r_{j-1} provides a rough check on whether r_j differs significantly from zero.[3] For the original series, r_1 through r_5 were more than twice their standard errors and hence significant at the 5-percent level. For $j \geq 6$, the r_j were less

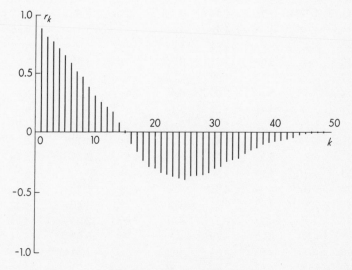

FIGURE 5 – 1   Sample Autocorrelations of Durand Annual One-year Spot Rates, 1900–1965

TABLE 5 – 1

The Durand One-year Maturity Spot Interest Rates and Conditional Expectations Computed from AR(2) and IMA(1,1) for Origin Dates, 1900–1967

Year, t	Spot rate, R_t	AR(2)					IMA(1,1), $_t\widehat{R}^*_{t+n}$
		$_t\widehat{R}^*_{t+1}$	$_t\widehat{R}^*_{t+2}$	$_t\widehat{R}^*_{t+3}$	$_t\widehat{R}^*_{t+9}$	$_t\widehat{R}^*_{t+35}$	
1900	3.97	—	—	—	—	—	3.97
1901	3.25	3.35	3.33	3.34	3.33	3.32	3.37
1902	3.30	3.29	3.30	3.30	3.30	3.31	3.31
1903	3.45	3.42	3.42	3.41	3.38	3.33	3.43
1904	3.60	3.56	3.55	3.54	3.47	3.35	3.57
1905	3.50	3.50	3.49	3.48	3.43	3.34	3.51
1906	4.75	4.49	4.44	4.37	4.05	3.47	4.55
1907	4.87	4.75	4.67	4.59	4.20	3.50	4.82
1908	5.10	4.95	4.86	4.77	4.32	3.52	5.05
1909	4.03	4.13	4.06	4.02	3.80	3.42	4.20
1910	4.25	4.16	4.11	4.07	3.84	3.42	4.24
1911	4.09	4.06	4.01	3.97	3.77	3.41	4.11
1912	4.04	4.00	3.96	3.92	3.73	3.40	4.05
1913	4.74	4.55	4.49	4.42	4.08	3.47	4.63
1914	4.64	4.56	4.49	4.42	4.08	3.47	4.64
1915	4.47	4.41	4.35	4.29	3.99	3.45	4.50
1916	3.48	3.60	3.57	3.55	3.48	3.35	3.64
1917	4.05	3.92	3.90	3.86	3.70	3.39	3.98
1918	5.48	5.14	5.06	4.96	4.46	3.55	5.24
1919	5.58	5.41	5.29	5.18	4.61	3.58	5.53
1920	6.11	5.85	5.71	5.57	4.88	3.64	6.02
1921	6.94	6.58	6.41	6.23	5.34	3.73	6.79
1922	5.31	5.39	5.24	5.13	4.58	3.57	5.55
1923	5.01	4.94	4.84	4.75	4.31	3.52	5.10
1924	5.02	4.90	4.81	4.72	4.29	3.52	5.03
1925	3.85	3.97	3.91	3.88	3.71	3.40	4.04
1926	4.40	4.25	4.21	4.16	3.90	3.44	4.34
1927	4.30	4.25	4.19	4.14	3.89	3.43	4.31
1928	4.05	4.03	3.99	3.95	3.75	3.41	4.09
1929	5.27	4.97	4.90	4.81	4.35	3.53	5.08
1930	4.40	4.44	4.36	4.30	4.00	3.46	4.51
1931	3.05	3.25	3.23	3.24	3.26	3.30	3.29
1932	3.99	3.82	3.81	3.78	3.64	3.38	3.88
1933	2.60	2.83	2.84	2.87	3.00	3.25	2.81
1934	2.62	2.66	2.70	2.74	2.92	3.23	2.65

TABLE 5 – 1 *Continued*

Year, t	Spot rate, R_t	AR(2)					IMA(1,1), $_t\widehat{R}^*_{t+n}$
		$_t\widehat{R}^*_{t+1}$	$_t\widehat{R}^*_{t+2}$	$_t\widehat{R}^*_{t+3}$	$_t\widehat{R}^*_{t+9}$	$_t\widehat{R}^*_{t+35}$	
1935	1.05	1.41	1.49	1.61	2.13	3.07	1.31
1936	.61	.85	.99	1.12	1.79	3.00	.72
1937	.69	.86	1.00	1.14	1.80	3.01	.70
1938	.85	.99	1.13	1.26	1.89	3.02	.83
1939	.57	.79	.93	1.08	1.76	3.00	.61
1940	.41	.63	.78	.93	1.66	2.98	.44
1941	.41	.61	.76	.91	1.65	2.97	.42
1942	.81	.93	1.07	1.20	1.85	3.01	.75
1943	1.17	1.27	1.39	1.50	2.06	3.06	1.10
1944	1.08	1.24	1.36	1.48	2.04	3.05	1.08
1945	1.02	1.18	1.30	1.42	2.00	3.05	1.03
1946	.86	1.05	1.18	1.30	1.92	3.03	.89
1947	1.05	1.18	1.30	1.42	2.00	3.05	1.02
1948	1.60	1.64	1.75	1.84	2.29	3.11	1.51
1949	1.08	1.72	1.81	1.90	2.33	3.11	1.59
1950	1.42	1.57	1.67	1.77	2.24	3.10	1.45
1951	2.05	2.05	2.14	2.20	2.54	3.16	1.95
1952	2.73	2.68	2.73	2.76	2.93	3.24	2.60
1953	2.62	2.68	2.72	2.75	2.92	3.24	2.62
1954	2.40	2.49	2.53	2.58	2.81	3.21	2.44
1955	2.60	2.62	2.67	2.70	2.89	3.23	2.57
1956	2.70	2.73	2.76	2.80	2.96	3.24	2.68
1957	3.50	3.38	3.39	3.39	3.36	3.33	3.37
1958	3.21	3.26	3.25	3.26	3.28	3.31	3.24
1959	3.67	3.58	3.58	3.56	3.49	3.35	3.60
1960	4.95	4.67	4.61	4.53	4.16	3.49	4.73
1961	3.10	3.36	3.32	3.33	3.32	3.32	3.36
1962	3.50	3.43	3.43	3.43	3.39	3.33	3.48
1963	3.25	3.29	3.28	3.29	3.30	3.31	3.29
1964	4.00	3.85	3.84	3.80	3.65	3.39	3.89
1965	4.15	4.07	4.03	3.99	3.78	3.41	4.11
1966	5.00	4.77	4.70	4.62	4.22	3.50	4.86
1967	5.29	5.12	5.02	4.92	4.43	3.54	5.22

SOURCE: One-year maturity spot interest rates: 1900–1942—Durand, *Basic Yields of Corporate Bonds;* 1943–1947—Durand and Winn, *Basic Yields of Bonds;* 1948–1952— *The Economic Almanac, 1953–1954;* 1953–1958—Durand, "Quarterly Series of Corporate Bond Yields"; 1959–1967—*The Economic Almanac, 1967–1968* (New York: National Industrial Conference Board, 1967. See footnote 3 in Chapter 2.

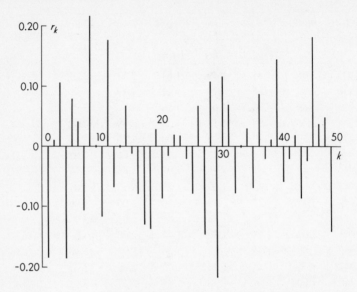

FIGURE 5 – 2   **Sample Autocorrelations of First Differences of Annual Durand One-year Spot Rates, 1900–1965**

than twice their standard errors and hence not significant. None of the sample autocorrelations were significant for the series of first differences.

Remembering that stationarity is characterized by the autocorrelations dying off with increasing lag, we note that for both $d = 0$ and $d = 1$ this is the case. The original series exhibits a very smooth damped wave pattern typical of second-order autoregressive processes. We note, however, that the smoothness and the wave shape of the estimated function are strongly influenced by the covariance between sample autocorrelations of the series. The approximate formula for these covariances is given by

$$C(r_k, r_{k+s}) \approx \frac{1}{n} \sum_{v=-\infty}^{+\infty} \rho_v \rho_{v+s}, \qquad (5.15)$$

where ρ_v is the theoretical autocorrelation of the series for lag v.[4]

We tentatively consider a second-order autoregressive process for this series, which may be written as

$$R_t - \phi_1 R_{t-1} - \phi_2 R_{t-2} = \theta_0 + u_t, \qquad (5.16)$$

where R_t denotes the one-year maturity spot interest rates. The theoretical relationships between the coefficients in $\phi_2(B)$ and the autocorrelations of the series may be used to obtain preliminary estimates of ϕ_1 and ϕ_2. These are given by

$$\widehat{\phi}_1 = \frac{r_1(1 - r_2)}{1 - r_1^2} = .76 \qquad (5.17)$$

and

$$\widehat{\phi}_2 = \frac{r_2 - r_1^2}{1 - r_1^2} = .16. \qquad (5.18)$$

Mixed processes are typified by having their autocorrelations tail off (exponentially for $p = 1$) after the first q irregular steps induced by the presence of a qth-order moving-average disturbance. Noting that $r_1/r_0 = .90$, while $r_2/r_1 = .935$ and $r_3/r_2 = .94$, we may reasonably entertain a mixed model with $p = 1$ and $q = 1$, which is written

$$R_t + \phi_1 R_{t-1} = \theta_0 + u_t - \theta_1 u_{t-1}. \qquad (5.19)$$

We obtain preliminary estimates

$$\widehat{\phi}_1 = \frac{r_2}{r_1} \approx \frac{r_3}{r_2} = .94 \qquad (5.20)$$

and from

$$r_1 = \frac{(1 - \widehat{\phi}_1\widehat{\theta}_1)(\widehat{\phi}_1 - \widehat{\theta}_1)}{1 + \widehat{\theta}_1^2 - 2\widehat{\phi}_1\widehat{\theta}_1}, \qquad (5.21)$$

we have

$$\widehat{\theta}_1 = .16. \qquad (5.22)$$

Considering next the empirical autocorrelations for the first differences, it is apparent that they do not fall into a neat pattern of tailing off or cutting off. Further, as mentioned previously, autocorrelations are well within the bounds of two standard errors. Hence we might well entertain the model

$$(1 - B)R_t = u_t; \tag{5.23}$$

that is, the first differences are white noise and the series is a random walk. If we consider $r_1 = -.19$ as some evidence for entertaining the model

$$(1 - B)R_t = (1 - \theta_1 B)u_t, \tag{5.24}$$

which says that the first differences are a first-order moving average, then from

$$r_1 = \frac{-\widehat{\theta}_1}{1 + \widehat{\theta}_1^2} \tag{5.25}$$

we have

$$\widehat{\theta}_1 = .20. \tag{5.26}$$

The preliminary parameter estimates in each of these models will turn out to be quite close to the final maximum-likelihood estimates and serve usefully as guess values for the iterative estimation program. While the three models proposed appear to be quite different at first glance, when written in equivalent form it is apparent that they are quite similar. Denoting the deviation of R_t from the mean of the process as $\dot{R}_t$, the tentative model AR(2) is

$$\dot{R}_t - .76\dot{R}_{t-1} - .16\dot{R}_{t-2} = u_t, \tag{5.27}$$

while the ARMA(1,1) model can be rewritten as

$$\frac{(1 - .94B)\dot{R}_t}{(1 - .16B)} = u_t \tag{5.28}$$

or

$$\dot{R}_t - .78\dot{R}_{t-1} - .12\dot{R}_{t-2} - \cdots = u_t \tag{5.29}$$

to the first two terms. The IMA(1,1) model becomes

$$\frac{1 - B}{1 - .20B} R_t = u_t \tag{5.30}$$

or

$$R_t - .80R_{t-1} - .16R_{t-2} - \cdots = u_t. \tag{5.31}$$

Comparison of the coefficients in the infinite autoregressive representations of these models, namely (5.27), (5.29), and (5.31), indicates little difference in their magnitudes. It is important to note, however, that while the first two models are stationary, the third is nonstationary. This distinction is important since if we choose a stationary form the process becomes "located"; that is, it has a mean value.

ESTIMATION OF PARAMETERS

Fitting the AR(2) model to the observations 1900–1967 yielded the following results:

$$R_t - \underset{(.1215)}{.7987}R_{t-1} - \underset{(.1224)}{.1338}R_{t-2} = .2237 + u_t,$$

$$\widehat{\sigma}_u^2 = .4694. \tag{5.32}$$

Estimated standard errors are given in parentheses under the coefficients, and $\widehat{\sigma}_u^2$ is the estimated value of σ_u^2. The t ratio for $\widehat{\phi}_2$ is 1.09, meaning that this coefficient is significant only at the 30-percent level. The t ratio for $\widehat{\phi}_1$ is 6.57 and is significant at the .1-percent level. The stationarity conditions for an AR(2) process are

$$\phi_2 > -1,$$

$$\phi_1 + \phi_2 < 1, \tag{5.33}$$

and

$$\phi_2 - \phi_1 < 1,$$

all of which are satisfied by the parameter estimates in (5.32).

For purposes of comparison, an AR(1) model was also run with the following results:

$$R_t - .9164R_{t-1} = .2770 + u_t,$$
$$\text{(.0519)}$$

$$\widehat{\sigma}_u^2 = .4700.$$

(5.34)

The coefficient $\widehat{\widehat{\phi}}_1$ is significant at the .1-percent level and appears to have "picked up" some of the weight given to R_{t-2} in the AR(2) model. The estimated correlation between $\widehat{\phi}_1$ and $\widehat{\phi}_2$ in the AR(2) model was $-.9056$, meaning that the sum-of-squares surface is relatively insensitive to changes in $\widehat{\phi}_1$ and $\widehat{\phi}_2$, which are opposite in direction.

This relationship is illustrated in Figure 5–3, where the negative orientation of the 90-percent confidence region for ϕ_1 and ϕ_2 is very apparent. Noting that the point $\widehat{\phi}_1 = 1$,

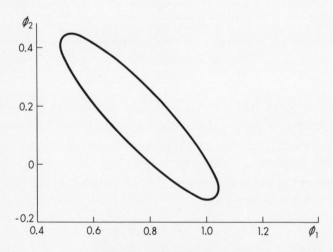

FIGURE 5 – 3   Ninety-percent Confidence Region for Parameters ϕ_1 and ϕ_2 for Model AR(2)

$\widehat{\phi}_2 = 0$ corresponds to the random-walk model,

$$R_t - R_{t-1} = u_t, \tag{5.35}$$

we see that this point lies on the edge of the 90-percent contour. Hence we may reject the random-walk model, the joint null hypothesis that $\phi_1 = 1$ and $\phi_2 = 0$, at approximately the 10-percent level.

As a further check on the autoregressive model, it was fit in overparameterized form with $p = 7$. Individual t ratios for $\phi_3, \ldots, \phi_7$ were all small. Since an observation is "lost" for each additional autoregressive parameter added, the error sum of squares for AR(7) was augmented by the reciprocal of the proportion of observations from AR(2) included in AR(7). This provided the basis for an approximate F test, which indicated no basis for the inclusion of $\phi_3, \ldots, \phi_7$. The adjusted F statistic so computed was smaller than its expected value.

The mixed model ARMA(1,1) yielded the following results:

$$R_t - \underset{(.0502)}{.9388} R_{t-1} = .2031 + u_t - \underset{(.1343)}{.1266} u_{t-1}$$

$$\widehat{\sigma}_u^2 = .4702 \tag{5.36}$$

While $\widehat{\phi}_1$ has a very large t ratio, that for $\widehat{\theta}_1$ is .94, indicating significance at only the 35-percent level. It is important to note that the models with moving-average parameters are nonlinear in the parameters so that tests based on classical normal regression theory are approximate and depend on the sum-of-squares surface being approximately quadratic in the parameters in the region of confidence intervals.

Since AR(2) and ARMA(1,1) are both subcases of ARMA(2,1), the latter provides an interesting basis for comparison as an overparameterization of both models. The fitted model ARMA(2,1) was

$$R_t - .7796R_{t-1} - .1521R_{t-2} = .2572 + u_t - .0188u_{t-1},$$
$$\underset{(.6821)}{} \quad \underset{(.6275)}{} \qquad \qquad \underset{(.6960)}{}$$
$$\hat{\sigma}_u^2 = .4760. \tag{5.37}$$

A comparison of coefficients among the three models is made in Table 5–2.

The correspondence between parameters of AR(2) and AR(2,1) is quite striking but in view of the size of standard errors should not be overemphasized. Nevertheless, this does provide some basis for saying that AR(2) better represents the behavior of the data.

Finally we consider the nonstationary model IMA(1,1) yielding

$$R_t - R_{t-1} = u_t - .1611u_{t-1}$$
$$\underset{(.1221)}{}$$
$$\hat{\sigma}_u^2 = .4676. \tag{5.38}$$

A t ratio of 1.31 for $\hat{\phi}_1$ is significant at approximately the 20-percent level. The relatively small distinction between this model and a random walk is apparent. Here again we may make a comparison in Table 5–2 with the parameter estimates

TABLE 5–2
Comparison of Parameter Estimates

	AR(2)	ARMA(1,1)	ARMA(2,1)	IMA(1,1)
ϕ_1	.7987	.9388	.7796	1
	(.1215)	(.0502)	(.6821)	(fixed)
ϕ_2	.1338	0	.1521	0
	(.1224)		(.6275)	
θ_1	0	.1266	−.0188	.1611
		(.1343)	(.6960)	(.1221)

from the ARMA(2,1) of which IMA(1,1) is a subcase. It is apparent that the fitted parameters of AR(2) are much closer to those of ARMA(2,1) than are the parameters of IMA(1,1).

Further, we may consider a comparison with the ARMA (1,1) model of which IMA(1,1) is a subcase ($\phi_1 = 1$). A t ratio test based on the deviation of the estimated ϕ_1 from unity indicates that the null hypothesis $\phi_1 = 1$ against $\phi_1 \neq 1$ may be rejected at approximately the 22-percent level. Since $\phi_1 = 1$ constitutes a stationarity boundary for ϕ_1, we consider the alternative hypothesis $\phi_1 < 1$, leading to rejection of the null hypothesis $\phi_1 = 1$ at the 11-percent level. Since the null hypothesis corresponds to IMA(1,1) and the alternative to ARMA(1,1), this test does provide some justification for preference of the stationary model ARMA(1,1) over the nonstationary model IMA(1,1).

While there may be some grounds for preference of AR(2) over either ARMA(1,1) or IMA(1,1) on the basis of comparison with ARMA(2,1) results, no sharp distinctions emerge between AR(2) and ARMA(1,1) on the basis of residual variance. In fact, scatter plots of the residuals from these models nearly correspond. In the light of comparison with ARMA(2,1) results, AR(2) was designated as being preferred to ARMA(1,1).

Since the ultimate objective of this study is the simulation of expectations of bond market participants, it was decided that experimentation with both stationary and nonstationary models would be useful—conditional expectations for future realizations of a stationary process converge with increasing horizon to the estimated mean of the series, while those for a nonstationary process do not converge to a fixed value but rather shift with the everchanging level of the series. Comparison of results from both might reasonably provide some insight into whether the market sees short rates as being

stationary. The work that follows draws on the AR(2) model
for the stationary case and the IMA(1,1) model for the nonstationary case.

COMPUTATION OF CONDITIONAL EXPECTATIONS

From our discussion of conditional expectations of
future realizations of a linear process in Chapter 2, it is
apparent that for the AR(2) process these are given by the
recursive relationship

$$_tR^*_{t+n} = \phi_{1t}R^*_{t+n-1} + \phi_{2t}R^*_{t+n-2} + \theta_0, \tag{5.39}$$

where for $n \leq 0$, $_tR^*_{t+n} = R_{t+n}$. The $\lim_{n\to\infty} {_tR^*_{t+n}}$ is given by some
$\bar{R}$ such that

$$\bar{R} = \phi_1\bar{R} + \phi_2\bar{R} + \theta_0; \tag{5.40}$$

hence

$$\bar{R} = \frac{\theta_0}{1 - \phi_1 - \phi_2}, \tag{5.41}$$

which is just the mean of the process.

To obtain conditional expectations implied by the esti-
mated process, denoted $_t\widehat{R}^*_{t+n}$, we replace ϕ_1, ϕ_2, and θ_0 in
(5.39) by their fitted values from (5.32), which yields the
computational formula

$$_t\widehat{R}^*_{t+n} = .7987{_t\widehat{R}^*_{t+n-1}} + .1338{_t\widehat{R}^*_{t+n-2}} + .2237. \tag{5.42}$$

Similarly, the estimated infinite horizon expectation is obtained by substitution of the fitted values into (5.41), yielding

$$\widehat{\bar{R}} = 3.3159, \tag{5.43}$$

which is also the estimated mean of the process. Thus, given any starting values R_t and R_{t-1}, the sequence of conditional expectations recursively from (5.42) approaches the estimated mean of the process, 3.3159. Actual computed expectations for horizons 1, 2, 3, 9, and 35 years and origin dates 1901–1967 are tabulated in Table 5–1.

The IMA(1,1) model is easily seen from our discussion in Chapter 2 to imply the following rules for computation of conditional expectations:

$$_tR^*_{t+1} = R_t - \theta_1 u_t \qquad (5.44)$$
$$_tR^*_{t+n} = {}_tR^*_{t+1}, \qquad n > 1. \qquad (5.45)$$

Since the profile of $_tR^*_{t+n}$ is horizontal, the value of $_tR^*_{t+1}$ may be thought of as the "level" of the series at time t.

Conditional expectations may be computed in practice using (5.44), replacing θ_1 by its fitted value and the u_t by the residuals, denoted $\widehat{u}_t$, given by solving (5.38) for u_t. Inserting estimated values in (5.44), we obtain the computational formulas

$$_t\widehat{R}^*_{t+1} = R_t - .1611\widehat{u}_t \qquad (5.46)$$
$$_t\widehat{R}^*_{t+n} = {}_t\widehat{R}^*_{t+1}, \qquad n > 1. \qquad (5.47)$$

From (5.38), we have

$$\widehat{u}_t = R_t - (R_{t-1} - .1611\widehat{u}_{t-1}), \qquad (5.48)$$

which, along with a zero value for the first residual in the sequence, permits recursive computation of the residual series. However, the expression in parentheses in (5.48) is simply the expectation $_{t-1}\widehat{R}^*_t$, and hence $\widehat{u}_t$ is seen to be the one-step-ahead forecast error $R_t - {}_{t-1}\widehat{R}^*_t$. This result corresponds to the equivalence between disturbances and one-step-ahead errors of conditional expectations established in Chapter 2. The computed forecast levels for the fitted IMA(1,1) model appear in Table 5–1.

Chapter 6 is concerned with the results of regressions that use conditional expectations implied by both the AR(2) and IMA(1,1) models as alternative measures of average expectations of market participants.

Notes

1. The methodology outlined here is developed in Box and Jenkins, *Time Series Analysis,* to which the reader is referred for a more detailed treatment.
2. *Ibid.*, Chap. vi., p. 177.
3. *Ibid.*, Chap. vi., p. 177.
4. *Ibid.*, Chap. ii, p. 35.

6

Testing the Term-premium Model by Simulation of Market Expectations

INTRODUCTION

A model for the determination of term premiums was developed in Chapter 4 from consideration of factors affecting the net supply of forward loans offered by risk-averse market participants. That analysis suggests that term premiums move inversely with the level of interest rates and with an index of business confidence. This chapter is concerned with testing those hypotheses primarily by simulation of market expectations as the conditional expectations implied by the fitted linear process models of Chapter 5.[1] The term-premium model may be expressed as [see (4.60)]

$$_t\widehat{T}_{t+n} = a_n + b_n I_t + c_n Z_t + \epsilon_{n,t}, \qquad (6.1)$$

where $_t\widehat{T}_{t+n}$ denotes the estimated term premium ($_t r_{t+n} - {}_t\widehat{R}^*_{t+n}$) and $\epsilon_{n,t}$ the compound disturbance ($w_{n,t} + f_{n,t}$). Our hypotheses imply that b_n and c_n are negative.

85

This chapter also presents tests of the specification of the linear process conditional expectations as measures of market expectations and of the specification of I_t and Z_t as determinants of term premiums rather than market expectations. The predictive content of the conditional expectations is also examined. Finally, the Hicksian liquidity preference theory is tested as an alternative to the term-premium model.

DESCRIPTION OF DATA USED IN TESTS OF THE TERM-PREMIUM MODEL

The Durand yield curve series provides interest rates of consecutive maturities from 1 through 10 years, and also 14-, 15-, 20-, 25-, 30-, and 40-year maturities annually from 1900–1958. The maturities through 10 years provided forward rates for consecutive 1-year horizons through 9 years. The longer maturities allow calculation of the 14-years-ahead forward rate, the 5-year forward rates for 15 through 19 years ahead, 20 through 24 years ahead, and 25 through 29 years ahead, and a 10-year forward rate for 30 through 39 years ahead. All available horizons were used at least experimentally at various stages of this study, although reported results are for the 1-year forward rates of consecutive horizons 1 through 9 years, and on the longest horizon, the 10-year forward rate of 30 years horizon. Estimated term premiums for 1 through 9 and 14 years ahead were computed as the difference between the forward rates and corresponding conditional expectations implied by the linear process models. The 10-year forward rate of 30 years horizon was treated as an approximation to the 1-year forward rate of 35 years horizon. The associated term premium was computed as the difference between this forward rate and the conditional expectation for 35 years ahead. This approximation allows us to proceed in the context of 1-year forward maturities and is a rather good approximation since the forward-rate and conditional expectation profiles are very flat in the 30- to 40-year horizon range.

The estimated term premiums were constructed using both of the alternative sets of conditional expectations presented in Chapter 5, namely those implied by the AR(2) model and those implied by the IMA(1,1) model. It may be well to recall at this point that the AR(2) model is a stationary process and as a result the profile of conditional expectations for given origin values approaches the mean of the process as horizon is increased. In the case of the 1-year rates used in this study, the 35-year-ahead expected rate varied little from the estimated mean of the process. The IMA(1,1) process, on the other hand, is a nonstationary process, no mean is defined, and the profile of conditional expectations is a horizontal line that defines a new level for the series at each time period.

In addition to forward rates computed from the Durand yield-curve series and the conditional expectations implied by the linear process models, we require a measure of the current level of interest rates, I_t, and an index of business confidence, Z_t, to complete the set of data needed to estimate parameters of the term-premium model given by (6.1). The choice for I_t was influenced by the desire to choose a measure of the current level of interest rates that was measured independently of the smoothed Durand data yet represented the yield on otherwise comparable securities. The yields on high-grade commercial paper of 4- to 6-month maturity were selected for these specifications and are tabulated in Table

TABLE 6-1

Yields on Commercial Paper, I_t, and Unemployment Rate, Z_t, 1901-1958

Year	I_t	Z_t	Year	I_t	Z_t
1901	5.00	2.4	1930	4.75	8.7
1902	5.25	2.7	1931	2.63	15.9
1903	5.60	2.6	1932	3.88	23.6
1904	5.75	4.8	1933	1.38	24.9
1905	4.71	3.1	1934	1.38	21.7
1906	5.79	.8	1935	.75	20.1
1907	6.50	1.8	1936	.75	16.9
1908	5.80	8.5	1937	.75	14.3
1909	4.22	5.2	1938	1.00	19.0
1910	5.16	5.9	1939	.56	17.2
1911	4.72	6.2	1940	.56	14.6
1912	4.50	5.2	1941	.56	9.9
1913	5.50	4.4	1942	.63	4.7
1914	4.38	8.0	1943	.69	1.9
1915	4.38	9.7	1944	.69	1.2
1916	3.50	4.8	1945	.75	1.9
1917	4.47	4.8	1946	.75	3.9
1918	5.88	1.4	1947	1.00	3.9
1919	5.13	2.3	1948	1.38	3.8
1920	6.38	4.0	1949	1.56	4.7
1921	7.63	11.9	1950	1.31	6.4
1922	4.88	7.6	1951	1.96	3.4
1923	4.63	3.2	1952	2.38	3.1
1924	4.88	5.5	1953	2.31	2.6
1925	3.63	4.0	1954	2.00	5.2
1926	4.25	1.9	1955	1.68	4.7
1927	4.13	4.1	1956	3.00	3.9
1928	4.00	4.4	1957	3.63	3.9
1929	5.50	3.2	1958	2.63	6.4

SOURCES: Commercial paper yields 1901-1942 are from Board of Governors, Federal Reserve System, *Banking and Monetary Statistics* (Washington, D.C.: U.S. Government Printing Office, 1943); and for 1943-1958 from the monthly periodical *Federal Reserve Bulletin* (Washington, D.C.: Board of Governors, Federal Reserve System). Unemployment rates are average annual rates for 1900-1947 from U.S. Department of Commerce, Bureau of the Census, *Historical Statistics of the United States* (Washington, D.C.: U.S. Government Printing Office, 1960); and the February rate for 1948-1958 from U.S. Department of Commerce, Office of Business Economics, *Business Statistics, 1967 Edition* (Washington, D.C.: U.S. Government Printing Office, 1967).

6–1. The February observation was used, since the Durand yield curves were developed from first-quarter data.

The selection of an index of business confidence naturally required a more arbitrary choice of variable. Business confidence presumably is related to the general level of business activity and thus the negative of the unemployment rate plausibly serves as such an index and is tabulated in Table 6–1.

ESTIMATION OF PARAMETERS IN THE TERM-PREMIUM MODEL

The classical least-squares estimates of coefficients in (6.1) using AR(2) conditional expectations in the construction of $_t\widehat{T}_{t+n}$ appear in Table 6–2. With the exception of $\widehat{b}_{35}$, all slope coefficients are negative in accordance with the analysis in Chapter 4. Although the coefficients are all several times their estimated standard errors, those standard errors are presumably biased toward zero owing to positive autocorrelation in disturbances, as evidenced by the Durbin–Watson statistics, denoted by D–W.

The classical least-squares estimates of coefficients in (6.1) using conditional expectations generated by the IMA(1,1) model appear in Table 6–3. The slope coefficients, including $\widehat{b}_{35}$, are all negative. The coefficient estimates are several times their standard errors, but the D–W statistics again suggest that these standard errors may be biased toward zero.[2]

The classical least-squares estimates reported in Tables 6–2 and 6–3 pose two econometric problems. One is the evidence from the D–W statistics of autocorrelation in residuals. The

TABLE 6 – 2

Estimates of Parameters in the Model

$$_t\widehat{T}_{t+n} = a_n + b_n I_t + c_n Z_t + \epsilon_{n,t}$$

Using AR(2) Conditional Expectations, 1901–1958

n	$\widehat{a}_n$	$\widehat{b}_n$	$\widehat{c}_n$	R^2	$D-W$
1	−.1331	−.0579	−.0238	.5571	1.1061
	(.0663)	(.0132)	(.0044)		
2	.2727	−.1094	−.0392	.6853	.9866
	(.0918)	(.0183)	(.0060)		
3	.3935	−.1432	−.0463	.7241	.9566
	(.1038)	(.0206)	(.0068)		
4	.4783	−.1596	−.0492	.7515	.9722
	(.1053)	(.0209)	(.0069)		
5	.6377	−.1836	−.0469	.7628	.9799
	(.1081)	(.0215)	(.0071)		
6	.7026	−.1882	−.0450	.7719	.9210
	(.1053)	(.0209)	(.0069)		
7	.7256	−.1817	−.0421	.7645	.7946
	(.1026)	(.0204)	(.0067)		
8	.8277	−.1900	−.0366	.7502	.7924
	(.1047)	(.0208)	(.0069)		
9	.8373	−.1841	−.0336	.7189	.7651
	(.1081)	(.0215)	(.0071)		
35	−.5898	.2072	−.0410	.5587	.3825
	(.1293)	(.0257)	(.0085)		

other is the probable existence of contemporaneous correlation between disturbances in different regressions within a set. It is reasonable to suppose that factors that cause some $_t\widehat{T}_{t+n}$ to deviate from its regression line would at the same time affect term premiums of other horizons. A technique for dealing with this combination of circumstances has been suggested by Parks.[3] He postulates a first- or second-order autoregressive process for the disturbances, which in the second-order case may be written

$$\epsilon_{n,t} = \phi_{1,n}\epsilon_{n,t-1} + \phi_{2,n}\epsilon_{n,t-2} + \gamma_{n,t}, \qquad (6.2)$$

where $\epsilon_{n,t}$ is the disturbance appearing in the nth equation and $\gamma_{n,t}$ is a serially independent disturbance, different for each n, which has expectation zero but may be contem-

TABLE 6 – 3

Estimates of Parameters in the Model

$$_t\widehat{T}_{t+n} = a_n + b_nI_t + c_nZ_t + \epsilon_{n,t}$$

Using IMA(1,1) Conditional Expectations, 1901–1958

n	$\widehat{a}_n$	$\widehat{b}_n$	$\widehat{c}_n$	R^2	D–W
1	.3370	−.1108	−.0209	.7291	1.1823
	(.0641)	(.0127)	(.0042)		
2	.6338	−.2040	−.0348	.8106	1.0225
	(.0909)	(.0181)	(.0060)		
3	.9056	−.2789	−.0410	.8412	.9781
	(.1075)	(.0214)	(.0071)		
4	1.1389	−.3355	−.0426	.8623	.9560
	(.1153)	(.0029)	(.0076)		
5	1.4328	−.3961	−.0394	.8697	.9542
	(.1263)	(.0251)	(.0083)		
6	1.6241	−.4348	−.0366	.8777	.8742
	(.1308)	(.0260)	(.0086)		
7	1.7654	−.4610	−.0330	.8779	.7713
	(.1360)	(.0270)	(.0089)		
8	1.9810	−.4998	−.0266	.8816	.7822
	(.1412)	(.0292)	(.0093)		
9	2.0955	−.5225	−.0229	.8805	.7597
	(.1466)	(.0292)	(.0096)		
35	2.0150	−.4965	−.0207	.9037	.9754
	(.1230)	(.0245)	(.0081)		

poraneously correlated across equations. Parks obtains estimates of $\phi_{1,n}$ and $\phi_{2,n}$ by fitting the individual regressions by classical least squares, obtaining the residuals from them, and then fitting regressions of the form of (6.2) using the residuals in place of disturbances. Substitution of the fitted regression (6.2) into the individual regressions yields the transformed equations

$$_t\widehat{T}^T_{t+n} = a^T_n + b_n I^T_t + c_n Z^T_t + \gamma_{n,t} \tag{6.3}$$

in which each original variable, say $X_{n,t}$, is transformed into $X^T_{n,t}$ by the relation

$$X^T_{n,t} = X_{n,t} - \widehat{\phi}_{1,n} X_{n,t-1} - \widehat{\phi}_{2,n} X_{n,t-2}. \tag{6.4}$$

The resulting transformed regressions given by (6.3) are then estimated using Zellner's efficient estimation procedure.

Instead of postulating the form of the process-generating disturbances, we applied the identification techniques described in Chapter 5 to residuals from the least-squares residuals. The sample autocorrelations suggested an AR(2) process for the disturbances. Instead of estimating $\phi_{1,n}$ and $\phi_{2,n}$ by regressions of residuals, we reestimated each regression in its transformed state, constraining coefficients so that unique estimates of each a_n, b_n, c_n, $\phi_{1,n}$, and $\phi_{2,n}$ were obtained.[4] The values of $\widehat{b}_n$ were little different from those reported in Tables 6–2 and 6–3 for the respective sets of conditional expectations, but the values of $\widehat{c}_n$ were smaller. Each $\widehat{b}_n$ in the two sets of regressions was significant at the .001 level, and the $\widehat{c}_n$ were significant at the .05 level for horizons 6 years and less in regressions based on AR(2) and for horizons 6 years and less in regressions based on IMA(1,1).

Using estimates of $\phi_{1,n}$ and $\phi_{2,n}$, transformed variables were constructed for two sets of ten regressions of the form of (6.3).

Computational constraints permitted "stacking" of only seven regressions and horizons 1 through 7 years were chosen. The efficient estimates of a_n^T, b_n, and c_n for the two sets of conditional expectations appear in Table 6–4.

The efficient estimates of b_n in Table 6–4 for AR(2) are negative and significant. The efficient estimates of c_n are also negative and significant. For the set of regressions using IMA(1,1), all coefficients are negative and each is significant at the .05 level, except for $\widehat{c}_7$, which is significant only at the .10 level.

TABLE 6 – 4

Efficient Estimates of Parameters in the Model

$$_t\widehat{T}_{t+n}^T = a_n^T + b_n I_t^T + c_n Z_t^T + \gamma_{n,t}$$

Using AR(2) and IMA(1,1) Conditional Expectations, 1903–1958

	AR(2)				IMA(1,1)		
n	$\widehat{a}_n^T$	$\widehat{b}_n$	$\widehat{c}_n$	n	$\widehat{a}_n^T$	$\widehat{b}_n$	$\widehat{c}_n$
1	.1524	−.0931	−.0166	1	.2622	−.1206	−.0133
	(.0440)	(.0166)	(.0054)		(.0486)	(.0153)	(.0051)
2	.2278	−.1775	−.0250	2	.4180	−.2175	−.0221
	(.0493)	(.0236)	(.0076)		(.0589)	(.0204)	(.0068)
3	.2656	−.2117	−.0291	3	.5283	−.2832	−.0264
	(.0529)	(.0264)	(.0084)		(.0647)	(.0231)	(.0077)
4	.2722	−.2256	−.0299	4	.6000	−.3299	−.0277
	(.0514)	(.0277)	(.0086)		(.0658)	(.0244)	(.0081)
5	.3165	−.2274	−.0267	5	.6617	−.3679	−.0244
	(.0533)	(.0274)	(.0086)		(.0680)	(.0263)	(.0087)
6	.2622	−.2192	−.0225	6	.5520	−.3837	−.0209
	(.0447)	(.0269)	(.0082)		(.0586)	(.0271)	(.0089)
7	.1941	−.1955	−.0160	7	.3264	−.3696	−.0161
	(.0367)	(.0260)	(.0079)		(.0468)	(.0288)	(.0095)

The empirical results presented in this section are thus generally consistent with the term-structure model developed in Chapter 4.

CHECK ON THE SPECIFICATION OF $_t\widehat{T}_{t+n}$

According to our specification of the estimated term premium $_t\widehat{T}_{t+n}$ as the difference between the forward rate $_t r_{t+n}$ and the corresponding estimated conditional expectation $_t\widehat{R}^*_{t+n}$, we may rewrite (6.1) as

$$_t r_{t+n} = a_n + b_n I_t + c_n Z_t + d_{nt}\widehat{R}^*_{t+n} + \epsilon_{n,t} \qquad (6.5)$$

in which $d_n = 1$ for all n. We shall adopt the convention of denoting coefficients that in theory are unity by d_n. Estimates of d_n may be expected to differ from unity if our specification of $_t\widehat{T}_{t+n}$ is wrong. Estimates of d_n may tend to be less than unity if the conditional expectations implied by either of the linear process models contain error as measures of the component of market expectations that is conditioned on the history of the 1-year spot rates.

Table 6–5 shows the results for such regression for representative horizons. The estimates of d_1, d_5, and d_9 in the case of AR(2) differ from unity by less than one estimated standard error. The estimate of d_{35}, however, is 4.94, suggesting that the 35-year horizon AR(2) expectation understates the movement in market expectations. If that is the case, the positive value of $\widehat{b}_{35}$ obtained in the corresponding term-premium regression may simply reflect the positive relationship between the forward rate $_t r_{t+35}$ and the level of interest rates.

TABLE 6 – 5

Estimates in Parameters in the Model

$$_tr_{t+n} = a_n + b_nI_t + c_nZ_t + d_{nt}\widehat{R}^*_{t+n} + \epsilon_{n,t}$$

Using AR(2) and IMA (1,1) Conditional Expectations, 1901–1958

			$AR(2)$			
n	$\widehat{a}_n$	$\widehat{b}_n$	$\widehat{c}_n$	$\widehat{d}_n$	R^2	$D\text{-}W$
1	.1138	−.0831	−.0232	1.0338	.9839	1.1380
	(.0713)	(.0359)	(.0045)	(.0447)		
5	.7278	−.1382	−.0481	.9225	.8929	.9547
	(.1533)	(.0587)	(.0073)	(.0933)		
9	.9546	−.1509	−.0345	.9278	.8078	.7461
	(.2220)	(.0588)	(.0073)	(.1191)		
35	− 12.3186	−.1640	−.0321	4.9475	.8943	.9056
	(1.3264)	(.0451)	(.0056)	(.4456)		
			$IMA(1,1)$			
n	$\widehat{a}_n$	$\widehat{b}_n$	$\widehat{c}_n$	$\widehat{d}_n$	R^2	$D\text{-}W$
1	.3490	−.0842	−.0216	.9668	.9850	1.1633
	(.0660)	(.0346)	(.0043)	(.0403)		
5	1.5507	−.1392	−.0467	.6781	.8966	.8966
	(.1093)	(.0573)	(.0072)	(.0668)		
9	2.2661	−.1509	−.0335	.5343	.8107	.7449
	(.1108)	(.0581)	(.0073)	(.0676)		
35	2.1695	−.1601	−.0302	.5783	.8930	.9259
	(.0860)	(.0451)	(.0056)	(.0525)		

There is little difference in estimates $\widehat{b}_n$ and $\widehat{c}_n$ reported in Table 6–5 as compared with corresponding term-premium regressions in Table 6-2, except that $\widehat{b}_{35}$ is negative in the former and consistent in magnitude with the $\widehat{b}_n$ of shorter horizon in contrast to its positive value in the latter.

Also $\widehat{c}_{35}$ is more consistent with the $\widehat{c}_n$ of shorter horizons in the forward-rate regressions.

The results for forward-rate regressions using the IMA(1,1) model casts differ markedly from those for the AR(2) model. The $\widehat{d}_n$ for horizons greater than 2 years differ from unity by more than two estimated standard errors. Although these standard errors are probably understated, it is clear that, except for the 35-year horizon, IMA(1,1) conditional expectations do not satisfy the specification of the estimated term premium as well as do those of the AR(2) model. Estimates of b_n reported in Table 6-5 are considerably smaller than corresponding estimates in Table 6-3 for term-premium regressions, and estimates of c_n are somewhat larger.

It is interesting that in these two sets of regressions that purport to explain forward rates, the coefficients of I_t and Z_t are nearly identical and close to the values reported in Table 6-2, whereas the coefficients of each set of variables $_t\widehat{R}^*_{t+n}$ are quite different. Since values of R^2 are nearly equivalent for the two sets of regressions, the low values of $\widehat{d}_n$ for IMA(1,1) may simply indicate that these conditional expectations, perhaps because of their shifting levels, exaggerate the movement market expectations.

TEST OF THE SPECIFICATION OF I_t AND Z_t AS DETERMINANTS OF TERM PREMIUMS

In the interpretation of the regressions presented thus far we have relied on the assumption that the variables I_t and Z_t are determinants of the term-premium component of forward rates rather than of the expectation component. One might well propose the hypothesis that the correct interpretation of regressions (6.5) is that the history of 1-year spot rates represents only part of the information incorporated in the expectation component of forward rates and that I_t and Z_t represent additional expectational information, rather than determinants of term premiums.

If this hypothesis is correct, then forward-rate forecast errors should be unrelated to I_t and Z_t. On the other hand, if the term-premium model is correct, then forward-rate errors should be negatively related to I_t and Z_t. To show this we denote by $\delta_{n,t}$ the error of the market expectation $_tR_{t+n}^*$ in forecasting the realized rate R_{t+n}, so that

$$R_{t+n} = {_tR_{t+n}^*} + \delta_{n,t}. \tag{6.6}$$

The term-premium model given by (4.58) may be rewritten in the form

$$_tr_{t+n} - {_tR_{t+n}^*} = a_n + b_nI_t + c_nZ_t + f_{n,t}, \tag{6.7}$$

where the left-hand side is the market term premium, $_tT_{t+n}$. Using (6.6) to substitute for $_tR_{t+n}^*$ in (6.7) and rearranging we have

$$_tr_{t+n} - R_{t+n} = a_n + b_nI_t + c_nZ_t + (f_{n,t} - \delta_{n,t}) \tag{6.8}$$

in which we have replaced the unobserved market expectation by the observable realized values of future spot rates, thereby obtaining estimated term premiums that are independent of estimated expectations. If term premiums are not related to I_t and Z_t, then $\widehat{b}_n$ and $\widehat{c}_n$ should be zero. However, if those variables are determinants of term premiums, then the term-premium model implies that $\widehat{b}_n$ and $\widehat{c}_n$ should be negative. Classical least-squares estimates of the parameters of (6.8) appear in Table 6–6. The 35-year horizon was omitted owing to the limited number of observations on R_{t+35}.

The pattern of D–W statistics in Table 6–6 indicates no evidence of serial correlation for $n = 1$ but increasing posi-

TABLE 6-6

Estimates of Parameters in the Model

$$_t r_{t+n} - R_{t+n} = a_n + b_n I_t + c_n Z_t + (f_{n,t} - \delta_{n,t})$$

1900–1958

n	$\widehat{a}_n$	$\widehat{b}_n$	$\widehat{c}_n$	R^2	$D-W$
1	−.3528	−.0237	−.0773	.4347	2.1787
	(.2005)	(.0399)	(.0132)		
2	−.4639	−.0612	−.1187	.5280	1.3423
	(.2632)	(.0523)	(.0173)		
3	−.5024	−.0920	−.1491	.6046	.8652
	(.2870)	(.0571)	(.0188)		
4	−.6709	−.0647	−.1683	.5516	.8636
	(.3491)	(.0694)	(.0229)		
5	−.5339	−.0836	−.1683	.4864	.6464
	(.4043)	(.0804)	(.0266)		
6	−.4929	−.0783	−.1678	.4313	.5434
	(.4484)	(.0892)	(.0294)		
7	−.5732	−.0444	−.1690	.3881	.4379
	(.4800)	(.0955)	(.0315)		
8	−.4267	−.0565	−.1600	.3364	.3647
	(.5148)	(.1024)	(.0338)		
9	−.5821	−.0098	−.1587	.2798	.2941
	(.5616)	(.1117)	(.0369)		

tive first-order serial correlation as the horizon increases. An explanation for this relationship may lie in the nature of the expectation errors, $\delta_{n,t}$. Let us suppose that the market expectation, $_t R^*_{t+n}$, may be thought of as the conditional expectation implied by a linear process (not necessarily one of the processes we have identified and fitted) given by

$$R_t = \mu + u_t + \psi_1 u_{t-1} + \psi_2 u_{t-2} + \cdots . \qquad (6.9)$$

The conditional expectation $_t R^*_{t+n}$ is given by

$$_t R^*_{t+n} = \mu + \psi_n u_t + \psi_{n+1} u_{t-1} + \cdots \qquad (6.10)$$

and hence $\delta_{n,t}$ is given by

$$\delta_{n,t} = u_{t+n} + \psi_1 u_{t+n-1} + \cdots + \psi_{n-1} u_{t+1}. \tag{6.11}$$

From (6.11) it follows that the covariance between successive errors is

$$E(\delta_{n,t+1}\delta_{n,t}) = \begin{cases} \sigma_u^2 \sum_{i=0}^{n-2} \psi_i \psi_{i+1}, & n \geq 2 \\ \\ 0, & n = 1, \end{cases} \tag{6.12}$$

where $\psi_0 = 1$. Our empirical analysis of spot rates suggests that the ψ_i may reasonably be assumed to be positive and hence that the covariance given by (6.12) increases with n as terms are added to the summation.

The estimate $\widehat{c}_1$ in Table 6–6 is negative and significant, while $\widehat{b}_i$ is negative but not significant. The signs of the $\widehat{b}_n$ and $\widehat{c}_n$ for $n > 1$ are negative for each n. Thus the results of this test do not provide statistically conclusive evidence, except for the highly significant value of $\widehat{c}_1$, against the hypothesis that I_t and Z_t represent only expectational information. However, the signs of parameter estimates are consistent with those implied by the term-premium model and with corresponding results from regressions using simulated expectations.

PREDICTIVE CONTENT OF TIME SERIES FORECASTS AND OF I_t AND Z_t

In the preceding sections we have considered various tests of our specification of conditional expectations implied by the linear process models as measures of market expectations and of I_t and Z_t as determinants of term premiums rather than of market expectations. In this section we shall examine the actual predictive content of the linear process expectations and of I_t and Z_t. Our first objective is to determine whether the computed expectations satisfy conditions reasonably assumed to hold for market expectations. Our second objective is to determine whether I_t and Z_t contribute, as additional variables, to the prediction of future spot rates in a way consistent with the hypothesis that they are determinants of the expectation component of forward rates rather than of the term-premium component.

One of the conditions required of estimates of market expectations is that they be unbiased, since we regard any bias in forward rates as term premiums. Over the 1901–1958 sample period the averages of the errors $R_{t+n} - {}_t\widehat{R}^*_{t+n}$ were .00, .01, and .04 percentage points for $n = 1$, 5, and 9, respectively, for AR(2); for IMA(1,1), the average errors were .00, .02, and .02.

Further, the ${}_t\widehat{R}^*_{t+n}$ presumably represent the conditional expectations of future spot rates given the past history of spot rates; that is, $E(R_{t+n} \mid R_t, R_{t-1}, \ldots) = {}_t\widehat{R}^*_{t+n}$. Thus in the regression equation

$$R_{t+n} = a_n^0 + d_{nt}^0 \widehat{R}^*_{t+n} + \delta_{n,t}^0 \qquad (6.13)$$

estimates of a_n^0 and d_n^0 should be close to zero and unity, respectively. Classical least-squares estimates of (6.13) appear in Table 6–7. The evidence of autocorrelation in disturbances is consistent with our discussion of forecast errors in the previous section. The estimates of a_n^0 in the set of regressions using the IMA(1,1) model are larger and the estimates of d_n^0 smaller than for the AR(2) model. These results reinforce our previous conclusion that the IMA(1,1) model is a second choice relative to the AR(2) model.

TABLE 6 – 7

Estimates of the Parameters in the Regressions

$$R_{t+n} = a_n^0 + d_{nt}^0 \widehat{R}_{t+n}^* + \delta_{n,t}^0$$

Using AR(2) and IMA(1,1) Conditional Expectations, 1901–1958

		AR(2)		
n	$\widehat{a}_n^0$	$\widehat{d}_n^0$	R^2	$D-W$
1	$-.0084$	1.0017	.8545	1.9062
	(.1957)	(.0552)		
5	.2042	.9326	.4491	.3681
	(.4746)	(.1380)		
9	.9494	.6949	.1539	.2249
	(.7351)	(.2177)		

		IMA(1,1)		
n	$\widehat{a}_n^0$	$\widehat{d}_n^0$	R^2	$D-W$
1	.2079	.9360	.8535	1.8614
	(.1858)	(.0518)		
5	1.0312	.6827	.4464	.3610
	(.3643)	(.1016)		
9	1.9373	.3967	.1510	.2216
	(.4507)	(.1257)		

We shall now consider further the possibility that I_t and Z_t are determinants of market expectations rather than of term premiums. Let us assume that market expectations properly incorporate any information about future realized rates contained in I_t and Z_t in the sense that the forecasting error associated with the market expectation is uncorrelated with values of those variables in the origin period. Suppose, then, that the market expectations is actually given by

$$_tR^*_{t+n} = a^*_n + b^*_n I_t + c^*_n Z_t + d^*_{nt} \widehat{R}^*_{t+n} + \epsilon^*_{n,t}, \qquad (6.14)$$

where $\epsilon^*_{n,t}$ is a disturbance incorporating the effect of other information. By combining (6.6) and (6.14), we obtain

$$R_{t+n} = a^*_n + b^*_n I_t + c^*_n Z_t + d^*_{nt} \widehat{R}^*_{t+n} + (\epsilon^*_{n,t} + \delta_{n,t}) \qquad (6.15)$$

where the compound disturbance in parenthesis is stochastically independent of the independent variables by assumption. Note that (6.14) is of the same form as (6.5), which was derived from the term-premium model, except that the dependent variable is $_tR^*_{t+n}$ in the former instead of the forward rate, $_t r_{t+n}$, appearing in the latter. If I_t and Z_t are determinants of market expectations, then estimates of the coefficients b^*_n, c^*_n, and d^*_n should resemble estimates of b_n, c_n, and d_n obtained by estimation of (6.5), which would then be viewed as explaining only the expectation component of the forward rate. On the other hand, if I_t and Z_t are only determinants of term premiums, and our specification of the linear process expectations as measures of market expectations is correct, then $\widehat{b}^*_n$ and $\widehat{c}^*_n$ should be close to zero and $\widehat{d}^*_n$ close to unity.

The values of $\widehat{b}^*_n$ and $\widehat{c}^*_n$ reported in Table 6-8 for the AR(2) model do not agree in sign with estimates of b_n and c_n in Table 6-5 obtained from regressions (6.5), but rather are all positive. The coefficient $\widehat{b}^*_1$ is not significant, whereas $\widehat{c}^*_1$ is significant. Thus the unemployment rate, Z_t, was a predictor of R_{t+1} during the sample period. However, its positive relation with R_{t+1} is inconsistent with the hypothesis that its role as a predictor accounts for its negative relationship to the forward rate $_t r_{t+1}$. The value of d^*_1 is not significantly different from unity. Nevertheless, the fact that the coefficient of Z_t is significant in explaining R_{t+1} suggests that information other than the past history of spot interest rates may help

TABLE 6-8

Estimates of the Parameters in the Models

$$R_{t+n} = a_n^* + b_n^* I_t + c_n^* Z_t + d_{nt}^* \widehat{R}_{t+n}^* + (\epsilon_{n,t}^* + \delta_{n,t})$$

Using AR(2) and IMA(1,1) Conditional Expectations, 1901–1958

			$AR(2)$			
n	$\widehat{a}_n^*$	$\widehat{b}_n^*$	$\widehat{c}_n^*$	$\widehat{d}_n^*$	R^2	$D-W$
1	.5326	.0268	.0518	.9181	.8884	2.2197
	(.2199)	(.1107)	(.0138)	(.1381)		
5	1.8145	.2240	.1130	.4464	.6323	.6978
	(.5316)	(.2036)	(.0252)	(.3235)		
9	3.5992	.4421	.1091	−.3418	.3745	.3823
	(.9999)	(.2650)	(.0328)	(.5366)		
			$IMA(1,1)$			
n	$\widehat{a}_n^*$	$\widehat{b}_n^*$	$\widehat{c}_n^*$	$\widehat{d}_n^*$	R^2	$D-W$
1	.7413	.0250	.0532	.8595	.8892	2.1944
	(.2099)	(.1100)	(.0137)	(.1282)		
5	2.2099	.2173	.1139	.3359	.6332	.6049
	(.3853)	(.2020)	(.0252)	(.2353)		
9	3.1165	.4433	.1087	−.1983	.3746	.3840
	(.5026)	(.2635)	(.0329)	(.3069)		

to explain future spot rates. This point underlines the simplicity of our expectation models.

Results for a set of regressions using the IMA(1,1) model also appear in Table 6-8 and are virtually identical to those reported for AR(2).[5]

In summary, these results do not support the hypothesis that it is the predictive content of I_t and Z_t that accounts for the negative relationship between estimated term premiums and these variables.

TEST OF THE LIQUIDITY
PREFERENCE THEORY

As an alternative to the term-premium model, we consider in this section the Hicksian liquidity preference theory discussed in Chapter 3. According to that theory, forward rates are given by

$$_tr_{t+n} = a'_n + {_tR^*_{t+n}}, \qquad (6.16)$$

where $_tR^*_{t+n}$ is the market forecast and a'_n is the Hicksian liquidity premium, L_n, which is invariant over time, positive, and increases monotonically with n. Thus the forward rate is viewed in this framework as a forecast with additive bias a'_n. Denoting as in (6.6) the forecast error of the market forecast as $\delta_{n,t}$, we obtain from (6.16)

$$R_{t+n} = -a'_n + d'_{nt}r_{t+n} + \delta_{n,t}, \qquad (6.17)$$

where, by convention, d'_n denotes a coefficient that theory predicts is unity. Consider next the expression

$$R_{t+n} = -a'_n - b'_n I_t - c'_n Z_t + d'_{nt}r_{t+n} + \delta_{n,t} \qquad (6.18)$$

in which variables I_t and Z_t have been added as independent variables with coefficients $-b'_n$ and $-c'_n$, respectively. If the liquidity preference theory is correct, then the true values of b'_n and c'_n are zero, and (6.18) reduces to (6.17). If the term-premium model is correct, then (6.18) may be interpreted as a rearrangement of (6.8), with one component of the dependent variable, namely $_tr_{t+n}$, transferred to the right-hand side and having coefficient unity. If the latter interpretation of (6.18) is correct, classical least-squares estimation will not provide unbiased estimates of the true parameters since, in (6.8), $_tr_{t+n}$ is correlated with the component $f_{n,t}$ of the disturbance.

Assuming first that R_{t+n} *is* the proper dependent variable, as specified by the liquidity preference theory, we note that the value of $\widehat{a}'_1$ in Table 6-9 is negative and significant, contradicting the prediction by the liquidity preference theory of a positive value for all a'_n. Further, the values of a'_n become increasingly negative with n. The value of $\widehat{c}'_1$ is negative and significant, which is at variance with the liquidity preference theory. The value of $\widehat{d}'_1$ is not significantly different from unity. However, the value of $\widehat{d}'_n$ declines with n and is negative for $n > 5$. If the stochastic specification of (6.8) is correct, so that $_tr_{t+n}$ is correlated with the true disturbance in (6.18), then we must regard the estimates in Table 6-9 as simply biased estimates of the true parameters.

Finally, if the liquidity preference theory is correct in specifying forward rates as market expectations plus a constant, and if those market expectations incorporate all relevant information, then the variances of forward rate errors $R_{t+n} - {}_tr_{t+n}$ should be at least as small as the variances of the linear process expectation errors. For the sample period,

TABLE 6-9

Estimates of the Parameters in the Models

$$R_{t+n} = -a'_n - b'_n I_t - c'_n Z_t + d'_{nt} r_{t+n} + \delta_{n,t}$$

1901-1958

n	$\widehat{a}'_n$	$\widehat{b}'_n$	$\widehat{c}'_n$	$\widehat{d}'_n$	R^2	$D-W$
1	−.4437	−.1124	−.0716	.8708	.8937	2.2660
	(.2186)	(.0942)	(.0142)	(.1242)		
5	−1.9823	−.4070	−.1183	.1949	.6226	.7428
	(.6390)	(.1373)	(.0306)	(.2852)		
9	−5.7061	−.5828	−.0639	−1.0814	.4464	.5004
	(1.0777)	(.1424)	(.0352)	(.3957)		

1901–1958, the variances of forward-rate errors were .53, 2.38, and 3.28 percentage points for $n = 1$, 5, and 9 years, respectively. In contrast, the corresponding error variances for AR(2) were .40, 1.56, and 2.45, respectively. For IMA(1,1) they were .42, 1.84, and 3.38, respectively. Error variances were smaller for both models at all horizons except that for IMA(1,1) at 9 years.

There would appear to be strong evidence in these results against the liquidity preference theory.

Notes

1. The statistical results presented in this chapter have appeared in Charles R. Nelson, "Testing a Model of the Term Structure of Interest Rates by Simulation of Market Forecasts," *Journal of the American Statistical Association* 65 (September 1970): 1163–1179.

2. To test whether the policy of pegging interest during the years 1942–1951 influenced term premiums, the regressions of Tables 6–2 and 6–3 were repeated with the addition of a dummy variable. Estimates for the coefficient of the dummy variable were of mixed sign and had small t ratios. Estimates of the other coefficients differed little from those reported in Tables 6–2 and 6–3.

3. See Richard W. Parks, "Efficient Estimation of a System of Regression Equations When Disturbances Are Both Serially and Contemporaneously Correlated," *Journal of the American Statistical Association* 62 (June 1967): 500–509.

4. A discussion of this and the method Parks proposed for estimation of $\phi_{1,n}$ and $\phi_{2,n}$ appears in E. Malinvaud, *Statistical Methods of Econometrics* (Skokie, Ill.: Rand McNally & Co., 1966), pp. 428–433 and 439–443. Malinvaud shows that both methods provide consistent estimates that have the same asymptotic efficiency.

5. As a check on the results of this section, the linear processes were refitted for subperiods 1900–1931, 1900–1941, and 1900–1951 and expectation series computed for the intervals 1931–1940, 1941–1950, and 1951–1958 using parameters fitted from data for the preceding sample subperiod. Thus computed expectations used only the past history of spot rates actually available to market participants on the origin dates. Repetition of regressions (6.15) for the subperiod 1931–1958 produced results that confirm those in Table 6–8. All values of $\widehat{d_n^*}$ for both models were positive, as were all values of $\widehat{b_n^*}$ and $\widehat{c_n^*}$ except for $\widehat{b_5^*}$, which was −.0534 with an estimated standard error of .3850. Values of $\widehat{a_n^*}$ and D–W were also quite similar.

Test of the Term-premium Model in an Error-learning Framework

INTRODUCTION

The error-learning model of the term structure discussed in Chapter 3 was originated by Meiselman as a device for testing the expectations theory. The parameter estimates he obtained appeared to be fully consistent with the expectations theory. This chapter begins with a reassessment of that evidence, which leads to the conclusion that the evidence may also be consistent with the existence of nonzero fluctuating term premiums. We also show that the term-premium model developed in Chapter 4 implies a respecification of the error-learning model to include the effects of interest-rate level and business confidence on the revision of forward rates. Estimation of parameters of the term-premium model in the error-learning framework leads to estimates that are close to those obtained in Chapter 6 by simulation of market expectations.

REASSESSMENT OF EVIDENCE FOR THE EXPECTATIONS THEORY FROM THE ERROR-LEARNING MODEL

The implications of the error-learning model may be enriched and the interpretation of empirical results sharpened by the introduction of theory pertaining to the formation and revision of expectations. We begin with the assumption that the market expectation consists of two components. The first, denoted $_tR_{t+n}^{**}$, is the expectation of the future spot rate, R_{t+n}, conditional on the history of one-year spot rates. The second, denoted $w_{n,t}'$, represents the effect of information that is independent of the history of spot rates $\{R_t\}$. Thus the market expectation is given by

$$_tR_{t+n}^* = {}_tR_{t+n}^{**} + w_{n,t}'. \tag{7.1}$$

If the sequence of one-year spot rates can be represented as a discrete linear stochastic process, then, using result (2.51), the conditional expectations $_tR_{t+n}^{**}$ are revised according to

$$_tR_{t+n}^{**} - {}_{t-1}R_{t+n}^{**} = \psi_n(R_t - {}_{t-1}R_t^{**}), \tag{7.2}$$

where ψ_n is the coefficient of u_{t-n} in (2.12), the pure moving-average representation of the process.

Allowing for the possibility that term premiums fluctuate over time and have a nonzero mean, forward rates are given by

$$_tr_{t+n} = {}_tR_{t+n}^* + (a_n' + f_{n,t}'), \tag{7.3}$$

where a_n' is a constant term and $f_{n,t}'$ denotes the fluctuating component of term premiums. Together, (7.1), (7.2), and (7.3) imply that forward rates are revised according to

$$
\begin{aligned}
_tr_{t+n} - {}_{t-1}r_{t+n} = {}&(a'_n - a'_{n+1} + \psi_n a'_1) + \psi_n(R_t - {}_{t-1}r_t) \\
&+ [(w'_{n,t} - w'_{n+1,t-1} + \psi_n w'_{1,t-1}) \\
&+ (f'_{n,t} - f'_{n+1,t-1} + \psi_n f'_{1,t-1})].
\end{aligned} \tag{7.4}
$$

Thus the revision coefficients for forward rates are seen to be the same as those for the conditional expectations implied by the linear process representation.

The disturbance term in brackets in (7.4) warrants attention before we proceed to the estimation of parameters. The independent variable $R_t - {}_{t-1}r_t$ is uncorrelated with the component $w'_{n,t} - w'_{n+1,t-1} + \psi_n w'_{1,t-1}$ by our assumption that the information incorporated in the w' terms is independent of the history of $\{R_t\}$. However, the independent variable is correlated, in general, with the component $f'_{n,t} - f'_{n+1,t-1} + \psi_n f'_{1,t-1}$ because $f'_{1,t-1}$ is a component of $_{t-1}r_t$ as well as because of the possibility that the f' terms may be correlated across time and horizon. Thus variation in term premiums has the effect of introducing *measurement error* into the independent variable with the consequence that least-squares estimates of ψ_n may not be consistent with estimates of the time revision coefficients. The amount of bias cannot be deduced a priori because of the range of plausible relationships among the terms involved. However, if the expectations theory is correct, then the measurement error is not present and least-squares estimates of the ψ_n should be close to the revision coefficients for conditional expectations implied by the linear process representation of $\{R_t\}$.

Least-squares estimates of the parameters of (7.4) appear in Table 7-1 for the Durand data over the sample period 1900–1958 and are nearly the same as those obtained by Meiselman for the 1900–1954 period.[1] The estimates of the constant term, $a'_n - a'_{n+1} + \psi_n a'_1$, are all small and not significant and thus are consistent with the expectations theory.

TABLE 7 - 1

Estimates of Parameters in the Model

$$_t r_{t+n} - {}_{t-1}r_{t+n} = (a'_n - a'_{n+1} + \psi_n a'_1) + \psi_n(R_t - {}_{t-1}r_t)$$
$$+ [(w'_{n,t} - w'_{n+1,t-1} + \psi_n w_{1,t-1}) + (f'_{n,t} - f'_{n+1,t-1} + \psi_n f_{1,t-1})]$$

1901–1958

n	$\widehat{a'_n - a'_{n+1} + \psi_n a'_1}$	$\widehat{\psi}_n$	R^2	D–W
1	.0039	.7089	.9089	1.7166
	(.0221)	(.0300)		
2	.0036	.5351	.7584	1.7700
	(.0297)	(.0404)		
3	−.0001	.4145	.6020	1.8540
	(.0332)	(.0450)		
4	−.0215	.3388	.4816	1.8416
	(.0346)	(.0470)		
5	−.0048	.2904	.4297	2.1926
	(.0329)	(.0447)		
6	.0022	.2447	.4085	2.3057
	(.0290)	(.0394)		
7	−.0078	.2492	.4168	2.1937
	(.0290)	(.0394)		
8	.0158	.2190	.3662	2.3869
	(.0284)	(.0385)		

They may also, however, be consistent with the existence of liquidity or term premiums under the special circumstances described in Chapter 3. The least-squares estimates $\widehat{\psi}_n$ are all positive and significant. Assessment of their consistency with the expectations theory requires, as we have suggested, comparison with corresponding coefficients for the revision of conditional expectations.

The linear process representations of $\{R_t\}$ developed in Chapter 5 provide alternative sets of implied revision coefficients, ψ_n, when they are rewritten in pure moving-average form. These are denoted $\widehat{\widehat{\psi}}_n$ and are tabulated in Table 7–2 along with discrepancies from least-squares estimates, $\widehat{\widehat{\psi}}_n - \widehat{\psi}_n$. Sampling error is, of course, present in all these estimates; however, the discrepancies are all positive and substantial in view of the standard errors of the $\widehat{\psi}_n$. This evidence of attenuation in least-squares estimates of the ψ_n suggests that term premiums as well as expectations may contribute to the movement in forward rates.

It is probably significant that the pattern of the $\widehat{\widehat{\psi}}_n$ implied by the AR(2) model is much more consistent with that of the $\widehat{\psi}_n$ and the discrepancies between them far less severe than is the case for the $\widehat{\widehat{\psi}}_n$ implied by the IMA(1,1) model. We note that the latter has appeared to be a second choice to the former on the basis of the representation of the series $\{R_t\}$ in Chapter 5 and on the basis of simulation of market expectations in Chapter 6.

TABLE 7 – 2

Values of $\widehat{\widehat{\psi}}_n$ Implied by Estimated AR(2) and IMA (1,1) Models and Discrepancies from $\widehat{\psi}_n$

	$\widehat{\widehat{\psi}}_n$		$\widehat{\widehat{\psi}}_n - \widehat{\psi}_n$	
n	AR(2)	IMA(1,1)	AR(2)	IMA(1,1)
1	.7987	.8389	.0898	.1300
2	.7718	.8389	.2347	.3038
3	.7233	.8389	.3088	.4244
4	.6810	.8389	.3422	.5001
5	.6407	.8389	.3503	.5485
6	.6029	.8389	.3582	.5942
7	.5673	.8389	.3181	.5897
8	.5338	.8389	.3145	.6199

TERM-PREMIUM MODEL IN THE
ERROR-LEARNING FRAMEWORK

The term-premium model developed in Chapter 4 is easily embedded in the error-learning framework as follows. According to the model, forward rates are given by

$$_t r_{t+n} = {_t R^*_{t+n}} + a_n + b_n I_t + c_n Z_t + f_{n,t}, \tag{7.5}$$

which along with (7.1) and (7.2) implies that the revision of forward rates is given by

$$\begin{aligned}
_t r_{t+n} - {_{t-1} r_{t+n}} = {} & \alpha_n + \psi_n(R_t - {_{t-1} r_t}) + b_n I_t \\
& + (\psi_n b_1 - b_{n+1}) I_{t-1} + c_n Z_t \\
& + (\psi_n c_1 - c_{n+1}) Z_{t-1} + [W_{n,t} + F_{n,t}], \quad (7.6)
\end{aligned}$$

where $\alpha_n = a_n - a_{n+1} + \psi_n a_1$ and $W_{n,t}$ and $F_{n,t}$ combine disturbance terms in the $w'_{n,t}$ and $f_{n,t}$, respectively.

Comparing (7.6) with (7.4) it is apparent that the contribution of the term-premium model has been the addition of the variables I_t, I_{t-1}, Z_t, and Z_{t-1} to account for variation in term premiums. If these variables account for all the variation in term premiums, then $F_{n,t} \equiv 0$ and measurement error has been eliminated from the disturbance term. Presumably, however, these variables account only for some of the variation in term premiums and therefore the possibility of bias in least-squares estimates remains. Consequently, we shall be interested in comparing estimates of the ψ_n with those implied by the linear process representations and estimates of b_n and c_n with those obtained in Chapter 6 by simulation of market expectations.

Least-squares estimates of coefficients in (7.6) appear in Table 7–3 for horizons 1 through 8 years. The estimates $\widehat{b}_n$ are all small relative to their standard errors and only $\widehat{b}_1$,

TABLE 7–3

Estimates of Parameters in the Model

$$_t r_{t+n} - {}_{t-1}r_{t+n} = \alpha_n + \psi_n(R_t - {}_{t-1}r_t) + b_n I_t + (\psi_n b_1 - b_{n+1})I_{t-1} + c_n Z_t + (\psi_n c_1 - c_{n+1})Z_{t-1} + (W_{n,t} + F_{n,t})$$

1901–1958

n	$\hat{\alpha}_n$	$\hat{\psi}_n$	$\hat{b}_n$	$\widehat{\psi_n b_1 - b_{n+1}}$	$\hat{c}_n$	$\widehat{\psi_n c_1 - c_{n+1}}$	R^2	$D-W$
1	−.0612	.7183	−.0354	.0532	−.0115	.0110	.9245	2.0129
	(.0622)	(.0592)	(.0404)	(.0340)	(.0070)	(.0079)		
2	−.1087	.5240	−.0210	.0504	−.0171	.0157	.7988	2.0792
	(.0839)	(.0799)	(.0545)	(.0459)	(.0095)	(.0107)		
3	−.1096	.3974	−.0123	.0404	−.0176	.0161	.6507	2.0714
	(.0961)	(.0915)	(.0625)	(.0526)	(.0109)	(.0123)		
4	−.2240	.2502	.0531	−.0012	−.0229	−.0203	.5868	2.3294
	(.0955)	(.0909)	(.0621)	(.0522)	(.0108)	(.0122)		
5	−.1522	.2311	.0457	−.0133	−.0142	.0094	.4773	2.3897
	(.0975)	(.0928)	(.0633)	(.0533)	(.0110)	(.0124)		
6	−.1242	.1805	.0654	−.0374	−.0109	.0071	.4527	2.5000
	(.0862)	(.0821)	(.0560)	(.0472)	(.0098)	(.0110)		
7	−.2150	.2089	.0699	−.0298	−.0066	−.0035	.4909	2.4757
	(.0838)	(.0798)	(.0545)	(.0459)	(.0095)	(.0107)		
8	−.1084	.1767	.0558	−.0299	−.0031	−.0018	.3976	2.4851
	(.0855)	(.0814)	(.0556)	(.0468)	(.0097)	(.0109)		

$\widehat{b}_2$, and $\widehat{b}_3$ are negative. The estimates $\widehat{c}_n$ are all negative but small relative to their standard errors, except for $\widehat{c}_4$. The D–W statistics reported do not provide strong evidence against the hypothesis that disturbances are serially uncorrelated.

Unrestricted estimation of Equation (7.6) ignores cross-equation constraints that are implied by the form of the coefficients of I_{t-1} and Z_{t-1}. If we denote the coefficient of I_{t-1} for horizon n as B_n and the coefficient of Z_{t-1} as C_n, then our deviation of the model implies the restrictions

$$B_n = \psi_n b_1 - b_{n+1} \qquad (7.7)$$

and

$$C_n = \psi_n c_1 - c_{n+1}. \qquad (7.8)$$

Since the restrictions run across equations and disturbances are presumably contemporaneously correlated across equations, a suitable test of their validity in the case of *linear* restrictions would be that suggested by Zellner in the context of efficient estimation of a set of regression equations.[2] To obtain linear approximations to (7.7) and (7.8), estimates $\widehat{b}_1$ and $\widehat{c}_1$ from Table 7–3 are inserted for b_1 and c_1 so that the restrictions actually tested are

$$B_n = (-.0354)\psi_n - b_{n+1} \qquad (7.9)$$

and

$$C_n = (-.0115)\psi_n - c_{n+1}. \qquad (7.10)$$

The test statistic for the set of eight equations is 1.3638, which is approximately distributed as $F(14,416)$ so that the hypothesis that the restrictions (7.9) and (7.10) are valid is accepted.

The restrictions may be used to sharpen our estimates of coefficients by applying Zellner's efficient estimation procedure subject to those restrictions. The computation required for restricted estimation rises sharply with the number of restrictions and number of equations. Results presented in

TABLE 7-4
Restricted Efficient Estimates of Parameters in the Model

$$_t r_{t+n} - {}_{t-1} r_{t+n} = \alpha_n + \psi_n (R_t - {}_{t-1} r_t) + b_n I_t + B_n I_{t-1} \\ + c_n Z_t + C_n Z_{t-1} + (W_{n,t} + F_{n,t})$$

1901–1958

n	$\widehat{\alpha}_n$	$\widehat{\psi}_n$	$\widehat{b}_n$	$\widehat{B}_n$	$\widehat{c}_n$	$\widehat{C}_n$
1	.0009	.7215	−.0307	.0300	−.0145	.0138
	(.0474)	(.0490)	(.0305)	(.0269)	(.0062)	(.0068)
2	.0086	.5782	−.0555	.0477	−.0221	.0188
	(.0505)	(.0533)	(.0279)	(.0272)	(.0067)	(.0075)
3	.0412	.4774	−.0682	.0486	−.0255	.0214
	(.0541)	(.0575)	(.0281)	(.0297)	(.0073)	(.0080)
4	−.0567	.4079	−.0655	.0606	−.0269	.0189
	(.0562)	(.0594)	(.0305)	(.0323)	(.0078)	(.0084)
5	.0223	.3983	−.0751	.0487	−.0236	.0136
	(.0608)	(.0631)	(.0332)	(.0364)	(.0082)	(.0094)
6			−.0630		−.0182	

Table 7–4 are therefore confined to horizons 1 through 5 years and implied estimates $\widehat{b}_6$ and $\widehat{c}_6$. The coefficients $\widehat{b}$ and $\widehat{c}$ are all negative and all are significant except $\widehat{b}_1$. None of the coefficients $\widehat{B}_n$ is significant, although their t ratios are all greater than 1. Four of the five coefficients $\widehat{C}_n$ are significant. Thus we find evidence in the restricted estimates consistent with the hypothesis that term premiums vary inversely with I_t and Z_t.

The estimated values of the constant terms are close to zero and, as in the case of Meiselman's regressions, none is significant. However, the significance of coefficients of I_t, Z_t, and Z_{t-1} provides empirical illustration of the proposition that zero constant terms are not inconsistent with the existence of term premiums. Estimates of ψ_n are larger than those reported in Tables 7–1 and 7–3 and are closer to the values in Table 7–2 implied by the AR(2) model of the one-year spot rates. These results are suggestive of a reduction in attenuation of estimates of the ψ_n as a result of the addition of variables that explain variation in term premiums. It is also interesting to compare estimates of b_n and c_n from Table 7–4 with corresponding estimates reported in Table 6–4 obtained by simulation of market expectations. The absolute values of the $\widehat{b}_n$ in Table 7–4 are smaller than estimates in Table 6–4 for both linear process models. However, estimates of $\widehat{c}_n$ in Table 7–4 are remarkably close to the alternative estimates of Table 6–4.

We conclude, then, that determinants of the term-premium component of forward rates may be incorporated into an error-learning model of the term structure. Evidence from the Durand data suggests that the level of interest rates and an index of business confidence are variables that affect the revision of forward rates in the way predicted by the model of term premiums developed in Chapter 4.

Notes

1. Meiselman, *Term Structure of Interest Rates*, p. 22.
2. See A. Zellner, "An Efficient Method of Estimating Seemingly Unrelated Regressions and Tests for Aggregation Bias," *Journal of the American Statistical Association* 57 (June 1962): 348–368. We note that for unrestricted estimation of Equation (7.6) least squares is efficient since the regressors in each equation are identical.

Summary and Suggestions for Further Research

SUMMARY

The objective of this study has been to develop and test a model of the term structure of interest rates. Chapter 2 was intended to introduce fundamental concepts including the empirical measurement of the term structure and the forward market implicit in a spot market in bonds of different maturities. Chapter 2 also presented a brief introduction to the theory of discrete linear stochastic processes, which we utilized extensively in our investigation of the role of expectations in the term structure.

The primary theories of the term structure and associated problems in empirical testing were outlined in Chapter 3. The role of expectations of future spot rates has been central to the development of term-structure theory and has provided the most difficult problem in empirical testing. We examined in detail the contention that the positive average slope of yield curves during the twentieth century constitutes evidence for the existence of liquidity premiums. We showed that the average differential between the longest and shortest maturity rates in the Durand data may be attributed to the effect of the serial correlation in short rates on the return to holding sequences of short-term bonds. Thus a positive differential need not imply the existence of liquidity premiums.

In Chapter 4 we developed a model of the term structure in the context of market participants considering forward contracts as alternatives to future lending or borrowing at uncertain spot rates. Risk-averse market participants were assumed to anticipate either holding a portfolio of loans or having to borrow in a given future period. Income in the future period depended on the forward position taken and on realized values of the spot rates and rate of change of prices. The relationships of the forward position to the expected value of income and to variance of income determined the choices of expected income and variance available to the participant. The net quantity of forward loans supplied to the market by a risk-averse participant was shown to increase with the term premium. The level of interest rates was introduced as a measure of risk that is related to the fact that the downward movement of spot rates is bounded at zero. The analysis suggested that the net quantity of forward loans supplied increases with the level of interest rates. An index of business confidence was included as an additional factor that increases the net quantity of forward loans supplied. The equilibrium term premium, that which clears the forward market, was shown to be negatively related to the level of interest rates and to the index of business confidence.

Chapter 5 contained the results of the identification and fitting of two discrete linear stochastic processes as models of the annual series of one-year rates in the Durand data. Testing of the term-premium model in Chapter 6 focused on the use of conditional expectations implied by these fitted linear processes as simulated market expectations. In regressions of estimated term premiums on variables representing the level of interest rates and an index of business confidence, the coefficients were negative, as predicted by the analysis of Chapter 4. Later sections presented tests of the specification of the estimated term premiums and of the explanatory variables as determinants of term premiums rather than of market forecasts. These results were consistent with the specification of the model. We also presented a test of the Hicksian liquidity preference theory and obtained results unfavorable to that theory.

Finally, in Chapter 7, we utilized the theory of discrete linear stochastic processes to derive an error-learning model for the revision of forward rates as a function of the current forward-rate prediction error and terms in the current and lagged values of the interest-rate level and index of business confidence. Resulting estimates of coefficients in the term-premium model were close to those obtained in Chapter 6 from regressions based on estimated term premiums.

SUGGESTIONS FOR FURTHER RESEARCH

In the area of theoretical development, important work remains to be done on the generalization of the maturity-choice problem facing individual participants. Expansion of the two-period forward-market model of Chapter 4 to include a greater number of periods and nonbond financial assets requires considerable complication of the analysis. Recognition of the opportunities for re-forming forward contracts in future periods implies that the problem should be cast in the framework of dynamic programming so that participants arrive at current decisions by working backward in time from some end point of the planning horizon. The presence of nonbond assets requires generalization of the concept of risk to account for the relationship of returns from forward contracts to those from other assets in the participant's portfolio.

Another important avenue of theoretical pursuit is toward the integration of term-structure theory with macroeconomic theory. In particular, the objective should be a general equilibrium framework in which short- and long-term rates are determined simultaneously with the other endogenous variables of the system. The most important results of such an analysis would be those relating to the flexibility of interest rates and the implications that follow for monetary and fiscal policy.

In the empirical area, perhaps the most interesting problem is that of finding more sophisticated methods for simulating market forecasts. The linear process models used in this study condition expected values of future interest rates only in the history of past rates. "Rational" expectations implied by the reduced-form equation for one-period spot rates from the kind of general equilibrium system proposed above would utilize more of the information available to the market. The success of this approach relative to the former would presumably depend crucially on errors of specification and estimation of the reduced-form equation. One might also investigate ways to incorporate information that signals changes in fiscal or monetary policy.

Clearly, much interesting and challenging work remains to be done.

Bibliography

Arrow, K. J. *Aspects of the Theory of Risk Bearing*. Helsinki: Yrjo Jahnsson Foundation, 1965.

Board of Governors, Federal Reserve System. *Banking and Monetary Statistics*. Washington, D.C.: U.S. Government Printing Office, 1943.

Box, G. E. P., and Jenkins, G. M. *Time Series Analysis for Forecasting and Control*. San Francisco: Holden-Day, Inc., 1970.

Aitchison, J. A. and Brown, J. A. C. *The Lognormal Distribution*. Cambridge: Cambridge University Press, 1963.

Culbertson, J. M. "The Term Structure of Interest Rates." *Quarterly Journal of Economics* 71 (November 1957): 485–517.

Durand, D. *Basic Yields of Corporate Bonds, 1900–1942*. Technical Paper 3. New York: National Bureau of Economic Research, 1942.

———. "A Quarterly Series of Corporate Basic Yields, 1952–1957, and Some Attendant Reservations." *The Journal of Finance* 13 (September 1958): 3–5.

Durand, D. and Winn, W. J. *Basic Yields of Bonds, 1926–1947: Their Management and Pattern*. Technical Paper 6. New York: National Bureau of Economic Research, 1947.

The Economic Almanac, 1953–1954. New York: National Industrial Conference Board, 1953.

The Economic Almanac, 1967–1968. New York: National Industrial Conference Board, 1967.

Federal Reserve Bulletin. Washington, D.C.: Board of Governors, Federal Reserve System.

Feldstein, M. S. "Mean-Variance Analysis in the Theory of Liquidity Preference and Portfolio Selection." *The Review of Economic Studies* 36 (January 1969): 5–12.

Goldberger, A. S. *Econometric Theory*. New York: John Wiley & Sons, Inc., 1964.

Grant, J. A. G. "Meiselman on the Term Structure of Interest Rates: A British Test." *Economica* 31 (February 1964): 51–71.

Hickman, W. B. *The Term Structure of Interest Rates: An Exploratory Analysis*. New York: National Bureau of Economic Research, 1943.

Hicks, J. R. *Value and Capital*, 2d ed., London: Clarendon Press, 1946.

Johnston, J. *Econometric Methods*. New York: McGraw-Hill Book Company, Inc., 1963.

Kessel, R. A. *The Cyclical Behavior of the Term Structure of Interest Rates*. New York: National Bureau of Economic Research, 1965.

Macaulay, F. R. *The Movements of Interest Rates, Bond Yields, and Stock Prices in the United States Since 1856*. New York: National Bureau of Economic Research, 1938.

Malinvaud, E. *Statistical Methods of Econometrics*. Skokie, Ill.: Rand McNally & Co., 1966.

Malkiel, B. G. *The Term Structure of Interest Rates: Expectations and Behavior Patterns*. Princeton, N.J.: Princeton University Press, 1966.

Meiselman, D. *The Term Structure of Interest Rates*. Englewood Cliffs, N.J.: Prentice-Hall, Inc., 1962.

Modigliani, F., and Sutch, R. "Innovations in Interest Rate Policy." *American Economic Review* 56 (May 1966): 178–197.

————. "Debt Management and the Term Structure of Interest Rates." *Journal of Political Economy* 75 (August 1967): 569–589.

Nelson, C. R. "Testing a Model of the Term Structure of Interest Rates by Simulation of Market Forecasts." *Journal of the American Statistical Association* 65 (September 1970): 1163–1179.

————. "Estimation of Term Premiums from Average Yield Differentials in the Term Structure of Interest Rates." Forthcoming in *Econometrica*.

Parks, R. W. "Efficient Estimation of a System of Regression Equations When Disturbances Are Both Serially and Contemporaneously Correlated." *Journal of the American Statistical Association* 62 (June 1967): 500–509.

Sutch, R. "Expectations, Risk, and the Term Structure of Interest Rates." Unpublished Ph.D. dissertation, Massachusetts Institute of Technology, 1968.

Tobin, J. "Liquidity Preference as Behavior Towards Risk." *The Review of Economic Studies* 25 (February 1958): 65–86.

Treasury Bulletin. Washington, D.C.: U.S. Treasury Department.

U.S. Department of Commerce, Bureau of the Census. *Historical Statistics of the United States*. Washington, D.C.: U.S. Government Printing Office, 1960.

U.S. Department of Commerce, Office of Business Economics. *Business Statistics, 1967 Edition*. Washington, D.C.: U.S. Government Printing Office, 1967.

Van Horne, J. "Interest Rate Risk and the Term Structure of Interest Rates." *Journal of Political Economy* 73 (August 1965): 344–351.

Wallace, N. "The Term Structure of Interest Rates and the Maturity Composition of the Federal Debt." Unpublished Ph.D. dissertation, University of Chicago, 1964.

Wood, J. H. "Expectations, Errors, and the Term Structure of Interest Rates." *The Journal of Political Economy* 71 (April 1963): 160–171.

Zellner, A. "An Efficient Method of Estimating Seemingly Unrelated Regressions and Tests for Aggregation Bias." *Journal of the American Statistical Association* 62 (June 1962): 348–368.

Index

Aitchison, J. A., 38

Ar, autoregressive process, 11, 67, 72–73, 76–82, 87, 90–96, 100–101, 103, 111

ARIMA, integrated autoregressive–moving-average process, 14, 67, 70

ARMA, mixed autoregressive-moving-average process, 13, 68, 76, 79–81

Arrow, K. J., 37, 49, 65

Bartlett's formula, 69

Box, G. E. P., 13, 17, 84

Brown, J. A. C., 38

confidence, business: as determinant of net supply of forward loans, 59; as determinant of term premiums, 96–108; index of, to estimate parameters of term premium model, 87–89

Culbertson, J. M., 19, 30, 37–38

default risk, as determinant of market yield, 1

Durand, David, *see* Durand yield curves

Durand yield curves, 5–6, 16–17, 21, 25, 27, 32, 65, 86–87, 89, 109, 116; one-year spot rates, 66, 70–74

Durbin-Watson statistics, 89, 97, 114

error learning, 10

error-learning model, use of: in testing expectations theory, 31–33, 35–36, 107–111

expectations: role of error-learning model in formation of, 31–33; role of, and stochastic processes, 9–16

expectations, conditional: computed from stochastic processes, 72–73, 82–84, 86–87, 89–93, 95, 101, 103

expectations theory, 18–20, 31–32, 36; and error-learning model, 108–111

Feldstein, M. S., 65

forward loans, 39; expected utility, 40–45; net supply, 59–60

forward rate, 6–9; definition, 6; for estimating liquidity premium, 34–35

future borrower, response of: to interest-rate level, 56–58

future lender, response of: to interest-rate level, 55–57

futures market in loans, 6–9

hedging, 44–45, 51, 56; future borrower, 57; future lender, 57

hedging pressure theory, 30–31

Hickman, W. B., 19, 37

Hicks, J. R., 21, 33, 37, 86, 104

IMA, integrated moving-average process, 70, 72–73, 77, 80–81, 83–84, 87, 89, 92–93, 95–96, 100–101, 103, 111

inertia hypothesis, 19

institutional theory, see hedging pressure theory

interest rates: as determinant of term premium, 96–108; to estimate parameters of term premium model, 87–88

interest rates, changes in level: as determinant of net supply of forward loans, 59; income and substitution effects, 56; response of future borrowers, 56, 58; response of future lenders, 55–56

Jenkins, G. M., 13, 17, 84

Kessel, R. A., 33–34, 36–38

liquidity preference theory, 20–28, 33; tests of, 22–28, 86,
    104–106
liquidity premium: cyclical movement, 33–36; existence of,
    20–28, 33, 110; and level of interest rates, 35
log-normal distribution, 24, 38

MA, moving-average process, 12, 67
Macaulay, F. R., 19, 37
Malinvaud, E., 106
Malkiel, B. G., 5, 16, 37
marketability, as determinant of market yields, 1
market expectations: business confidence as determinant of,
    101–102; current level of interest rates as determinant
    of, 101–102; measurement, 64–65; simulation of, as test
    of term premium model, 85–106
maturity-choice problem, 39
Meiselman, D., 17, 31–33, 35–36, 38, 107, 109, 115–116
Modigliani, F., 28–30, 37–38

Nelson, Charles R., 37, 106

Operation Twist, 29

Parks, R. W., 90, 92, 106
preferred habitat theory, 28–30

risk: aversion, 20, 37, 49; averter, 42; index of subjective, 53 speculator, response of: to interest-rate level, 56

spot loans, 39

spot rates, expectations of future, 9

stochastic processes: autocorrelation function, 68; estimation
of parameters, 67–70, 76, 80; identification of models,
67–70; theory of, 9, *see also* AR, ARIMA, ARMA,
IMA, MA

supply functions, aggregation of individual, 60–64

Sutch, R., 28–30, 37–38

tax structure, as determinant of market yields, 1

Taylor series, 42

term premium: definition, 2, 40; as determinant of net
supply of forward loans, 59; estimates of, 87; income
and substitution effects, 46–52; response to changes in,
46–52

term premium model: estimation of parameters, 87, 89–95,
98, 101, 103, 113, 115; testing of, by simulation of
market expectations, 85–106; test of, in error-learning
framework, 107–116

term to maturity, 1, 3; as determinant of market yields, 1

term structure of interest rates: definition, 1; measurement,
3–6; methodology, 18–38; model of cyclical movement,
39–65; theory, 18–38

Tobin, J., 43, 65

U.S. Treasury securities, yield curves, 5–6

utility function, 41

Van Horne, Jr., 17, 33, 35–36, 38

Wallace, N., 4, 16

Winn, W. J., 17

Wood, J. H., 33, 38

yield curves: for high-grade corporate bonds, 5–6; for U.S.
    Treasury securities, 5–6
yield to maturity, 4–6; definition, 4

Zellner, A., 92, 114, 116